SEARCHING FOR IRINA

Misha Feigin

Dreaming People Publishing

PRAISE FOR SEARCHING FOR IRINA

"Searching for Irina take us on a wonderful journey. It has so many layers and Feigin's writing style allows the reader to experience each scene, detail and location in a completely unique way. Searching for Irina is riveting and immersive, extremely well done."

- Colin Graham, President Graham Publishing Group

"Misha Feigin searches in this book both for Irina, the lover of his young adult years in Moscow, and for the "Peace" that the Greek origin of her Russian name promises. This journey takes us through public baths, disappearing pubs, idyllic woodlands, raucous parties, and cat-and-mouse encounters with the Brezhnev-era Soviet asylum system that was as warped as Kesey's "Cuckoo's Nest." You will find joy, greed, tears, terror, kindness, generosity, and cruelty. Sometimes they mix disturbingly like a Francis Bacon canvas. Sometimes they clang with the balance of contrasts in a Rothko. What you will not find are simplified answers. Feigin respects both love and words too much for such."

- Quinn T. Chipley, M.D. Retired from a practice in psychology, and Humanities Ph.D. focusing on William Faulkner

"Read these stories and discover what Bohemian life in the Soviet era Moscow was actually like. In the tradition of Miller, Celine and Kerouac, a young man discovers his artistic self in these stories of drugs, alcohol and love."

*- **Harold Maier, the founder of Twice Told Books***

Copyright © 2022 by Misha Feigin.

All rights reserved. No part of this book may be reproduced in any written, electronic, recording, or photocopying without written permission of the publisher or author. The exception would be in the case of brief quotations embodied in articles or reviews and pages where permission is specifically granted by the publisher or author.

Misha Feigin/Dreaming People Publishing
221 N. Clifton # 31, Louisville, KY 40206 USA

Printed in the United States of America

Front cover drawing by Irina Nikolaevna Radina from her prison notebook
Cover design by Ben Jones and James Oaks
Back cover photo of Misha by Boris Kaplinski
Author Photo by David Green
Poetry by Misha Feigin

Although every precaution has been taken to verify the accuracy of the information contained herein, the author and publisher assume no responsibility for any errors or omissions. No liability is assumed for damages that may result from the use of information contained within.

Searching For Irina/ Misha Feigin -- 2nd revised ed.

CONTENTS

Election Day 1

Tripping Over Freedom 5

One Baldy and Lenin Time 13

Soldier 21

The Dance 27

God Loves Sex and Books 37

Cohen's Arrest 53

Searching for Irina 85

Acknowledgements

I would like to thank Quinn Chipley and Cindy Rayner for their generous help that allowed me to complete this book.

PREFACE

I moved from Moscow to New York City in 1990, one year before the USSR fell. After that tectonic shift, the Russian underground culture collapsed together with its official counterpart. The brave new world was looming and I wanted to tell stories of Russian nonconformists I knew before the memories faded.

Sex, drugs and rock n' roll penetrated the Iron Curtain in the early seventies. My friends and I joyfully embraced this novel lifestyle. We grew long hair, bought American blue jeans and rock n' roll records on the black market, and watched forbidden films on a few VCRs available in friends' packed living rooms. We hung out in artistic squats, attended unofficial house concerts and exhibits, and read banned books. We learned how to be subversive and invisible at the same time so we could evade Big Brother's attention. Duping the authorities was an exhilarating experience, a useful approach in the dark times.

The characters in this book are real people. All events took place. All names have been changed.

- Misha Feigin

ELECTION DAY

On this special day, gleaming Manya emerged from her room dressed in her very best. At six in the morning, everything was still quiet in the Moscow communal apartment № 9 in house № 24 on Kropotkin - yes, the forefather of anarchism – street.

The communal apartment, in this particular case, housed 17 neighbors occupying six rooms, offering all a small toilet, a bathroom, and a kitchen. There were two gas stoves in the kitchen, and each family had an assigned burner. Any deviant recklessly disregarding this arrangement was eventually confronted by an angry neighbor whose burner was violated. The ostracism of the community followed.

The toilet was perpetually occupied. If you spent more than three minutes in this place of leisure, you would hear someone knocking at the door at any time demanding freedom to use the toilet, equality for all guts, and brotherhood among all neighbors with essential urges.

I had seen these words – freedom, equality and brotherhood – because they were printed in big, fat letters on a huge red banner below three bearded heads, two hairy ones and one bald.

The heads were of Karl Marx, Frydrych Engels, and Vladimir Ilyich Lenin, the bald one. On major holidays, such as Revolution Day, Victory Day, and the First of May, the three-heads banner hung down from the Fine Arts Academy building, one of the finest classical palaces of Moscow, a five-floor 19th Century apartment building that looked also quite nice from the outside. It was directly across the street from our home.

I can remember the banner as early as 1957 when I learned how to read slogans. It originally had four heads, but one – beardless, with the famous mustache – was removed sometime after Khrushchev's secret speech denouncing Stalin in 1956.

It was Election Day, and my nanny, as usual, was ready to vote early in the morning. Like many other country girls, she came to Moscow in the late 1920s in search of a better life. They fled their villages after the bloody civil war and the famine that followed it. Manya ended up becoming my mother's nanny. She lived in a tiny room that had originally been used as a storage room. My grandfather was able to obtain a permit for her to move in after a long struggle with some unyielding local authorities. Manya's bed was on top of the iron chest that held most of her possessions.

On every Election Day, Manya was ready to vote, ever gleaming with excitement. She always arrived at a polling station a few minutes before it opened. She wanted to be the first citizen in her district to cast a ballot, and – maybe – to have her picture taken for a newspaper.

"The very first citizen fulfilling her civic duties at the Kropotkin polling district was… "

My mother, in the course of telling me this dramatic story, never mentioned if Manya actually was ever photographed for a newspaper. I hope she was, because she sincerely believed in everything the radio said.

Manya could not write or read, so at the polling station, she normally excused herself with a polite statement: "I'm sorry! I'm afraid I left my *pince-nez* at home," before asking someone to print her name on the ballot.

Manya died in 1954 when I was just three years old. But amazingly, I remember her, one of my first memories, walking into our room – a crispy white shirt and the neatly arranged gray hair – announcing proudly: "I've already voted!"

Ten years later I found out from an older girl I was in love with that all elections in my country were for one part, one candidate. The only party was the Communist Party of the USSR, or just the Party.

Dar, Beloved, and Cincinnatus

TRIPPING OVER FREEDOM

Andrei Darmenkov, or Dar as we called him, was a slight, agile man in his twenties with a wild stack of curly hair. His eyes were usually hidden behind John Lennon-style dark glasses hanging miraculously at the tip of his nose. When Dar took off his glasses, everyone could clearly see how stoned he was.

One of the first and most noted hippies in Moscow, Dar did everything just right according to his honorable status. I can't recall a single time when he wasn't appropriately drunk or high on drugs.

Getting high on drugs was considered a crime because of the never-ending class struggle in our society. When you were stoned, you exposed your inferior class origin. The proletarians belonging to the ruling class were supposed to consume alcohol only for their recreation. Drinking alcohol profusely was a minor misdemeanor, even if you were a stinking hooligan puking all over the place.

Dar never looked like or acted as a puking hooligan, but his appearance and attitude always led him into trouble. He had a unique relationship with authorities, especially with the police. To say cops and Dar resented each other doesn't even come close to describing the level of animosity displayed at every encounter they had.

The process always started on both ends simultaneously. If Dar and cops simply saw each other on the same street, they rushed immediately towards each other with Dar beginning to shout: "You, fascists!" and cops apprehending him as swiftly as possible without saying a word. It was a rule.

Another rule was his habit of being late for rock'n'roll events that were quite abundant in our underground existence. Once, just a few minutes after a popular fusion band Arsenal had finished playing, Dar showed up in his dark glasses. Nothing could hide that he was even more stoned than usual. Dar stumbled and barely could speak, but he still proceeded directly to the band leader, shook his hand, and, overcoming his speech impediment, pronounced: "Uh, Ah, it was great, man!"

Dar loved rock music fanatically. He was one of the few in our gang who knew English and could recite at any time Jimi Hendrix, Beatles, or Rolling Stone lyrics.

It was difficult to believe that his father was the Second Party Secretary of the Leningradsky District of Moscow. And it was difficult to believe looking at his shaking hands and perpetually unfocused features that he had a master degree in geography and English.

He could have joined the Party and had a career, but Dar had a pristine soul and gentle heart.

He had chosen Jimi Hendrix instead, once and forever.

You could learn everything you wanted to know about Russian drug culture by simply observing Dar's life. He tried and used everything he could lay his hands on. First, it was codeine. Then he learned that adding two pills of the Hungarian tranquilizer Noxiron to six codeine pills led to much more gratifying and consistent results. The codeine period was followed by the longer codenox period. In these early days we obtained most of our substances from drug stores, so adventures with fake prescriptions were very common.

According to a legend, a notorious Moscow drug addict, Ghera, once showed up at a local drugstore with an antique sword awarded to his grandfather who served in the cavalry during the Civil War. In addition to the sword he was waving frantically, Ghera carried a prescription for both Codeine and Noxiron, an absolutely implacable combination for one prescription.

"You bastards!" he shouted, "Fill my prescription right away! I am a fucking Civil War veteran!"

Everyone in the drugstore was paralyzed with laughter, so Ghera was able to bolt before cops arrived.

Most of us eventually ran into trouble trying to fill our prescriptions, but Dar himself was a trouble for his mighty father who had to rescue him on a regular basis.

Like all fathers, the Party Secretary still dreamed of his prodigal son's resurrection, so he found Dar a job teaching scientific atheism at the Supreme Party Courses. This discipline was supposed to provide solid proof that no gods ever existed.

We were thrilled to hear Dar's Jesus stories. He examined his students in the spirit of all-forgiveness.

"Then I asked this idiot when Jesus Christ was born. She stayed silent and looked at me bug-eyed, so I asked, 'Who was Jesus Christ?'

"She told me Jesus was an astronaut. The girl learned it reading Science and Religion magazine. I gave her a passing grade."

Another important period in Dar's life was his Substance period – a new, ingeniously simple, and excessive drug. Substance was invented by some unknown genius in the 1970s when drugstores clamped down on fake prescriptions.

You could produce generous amounts of Substance by using a test-tube, a napkin serving as a filter, and three cheap, harmless ingredients: vinegar, magnesium crystals, and ephedrine, easily available as a cough medication in drugstores. If you did everything right, the final result of your chemical labors was a transparent liquid with a slightly sour taste and no smell. Legally, it was not considered a drug at that time. However, police still could bust you for having or producing it. Of course, if they really wanted you, they could plant something more appropriate in your kitchen drawer.

Substance was a stimulant. After you took it, your brain began to work in overdrive. You could talk without stopping for hours. All sorts of ideas and speculations just poured out of your mouth.

I remember once, during the Moscow International Animation Festival, a rumor spread that the Beatles' Yellow Submarine was showing. Of course, all tickets were sold out in a few hours, so we had to be really creative in trying to get in. My air-conditioning colleague and I arrived at the theater wearing work uniforms and carrying a long ladder and shoulder bags with heavy wrenches. Accommodating ticket takers threw the doors wide open and led us to the bathrooms, where we shed our uniform jackets, stashed the ladder and bags with wrenches and quietly walked into the theater where the film had just started.

Dar acted in a more simple and honorable fashion. He took an extra dose of Substance and just serenely walked pass the ticket takers. Maybe, observing his worn-out denim attire and round, dark glasses, they mistook him for one of these eccentric foreigners; or perhaps, he simply became invisible.

Dar was on Substance all the time. The concoction was not addictive physically, but he somehow managed to get hooked on it. After a year of using it, he ate and slept very little. He became a shadow in the wind. He managed to survive this drug just like he survived other sweet things of the dark. He lived through it all. However, the trouble was that a big part of his brain was gone, burnt out.

After all his experimentation with various substances, Dar finally discovered his drug of choice, as gentle and harmless as himself. It was milk. Dar began getting high on milk.

It was fascinating! He joined our drinking rituals with only one humble plea: "Would you get me some milk?" Of course, he always got it – 32 kopeks for half a liter, a deal!

Dar drank milk slowly, frequently stopping and licking his lips. He usually got visibly high after finishing the first carton. After we finished our drinks and Dar was through with his milk, you couldn't tell who was having more fun.

I haven't heard any news about Dar since the time I left Moscow. I hope he is still alive and still getting his milk. Or maybe he has learned how to get high on air. As long as he is breathing…

Vladimir Ilyich Lenin pointing at 11 a.m. on a one-ruble coin

ONE BALDY AND LENIN TIME

A dreary Moscow winter morning. The light snow made the city look unfocused, dreamy. The soft, white powder continued to float from the low, gray sky. Haziness clouded faces in the busy crowd spilling from buses and subway entrances onto sidewalks.

The time was 10:45 a.m. and there was no uncertainty among our ranks at the worksite. We belonged to a funky tribe of construction workers, plumbers, electricians and machinery operators. I and a few other engineers were also accepted into the brotherhood. There were other friendly tribes practicing the same ritual: lab technicians, factory workers, various clerks and other blue-collar folk. The ritual was pretty much the same in all tribes:

"How much have you got?"

"Two baldies."

"Well, I have one and some change."

We were in a hurry because it was ten minutes before Lenin Time, and the same ritual occurred all over our capital city, and in fact, across all eleven time zones with which

Russia was blessed. I am certain each had its Lenin Time that signaled a screeching stop for most industrial and administrative activities.

My boss pulled out of his shabby work pants a shiny one-ruble coin, which shows Lenin's statue with his outstretched right hand pointing to our radiant communist future.

Our chieftain swiftly placed the coin on top of his wristwatch. We held our breath. Our forefather's hand pointed exactly at 11 a.m. It meant that all liquor stores were now open. We hastily pooled our money. It was Lenin Time!

The two baldies I contributed for our common good were great coins – you could rub Lenin's bald head with your thumb – it felt pleasant and calming. Some bold observers claimed that if you turned the coin upside down, you could see a disguised wine glass in Lenin's triangular beard. I was never sure about that because my baldies disappeared fast. They were well spent on vodka or, when our assets were insufficient, on nasty rotgut preposterously called port – a very popular drink in our country. It was represented by a variety of brands, but the taste of each one was equally disgusting.

But any taste was fine with us when we enjoyed ourselves during an extended lunch break.

Normally, right before Lenin Time our cash was passed to a messenger – the one whose pants were cleaner than those of the others, because a sign on the wall of every liquor store warned "persons in work clothes will not be served." This rule was strictly enforced. It was supposed to keep our proletariat from excessive drinking at work. So, if you wanted to buy any alcohol around Lenin Time, you would get a decent chance to be successful if you looked like a peaceful vacationer or a harmless administrator. Compassion, however, was always present in the mysterious Russian soul – just ask Dostoevsky!

In case of an emergency, you could always pass your money to some appropriately attired kindred spirit and get your merchandise outside, right by the store's door. Not so seldom, you'd be drinking together in a few minutes in some nearby park or a secluded yard.

As an engineer, and thus one with cleaner pants, I was often blessed with the task of acting as a messenger. On that day I was at my designated place in the restless vodka line with my pocket full of baldies, crumpled one ruble bills and some change.

The liquor store was a tough place around Lenin Time. But in the middle of all that pushing and shoving, sympathy could shine its soft light onto the thirsty, anxious crowd. Women who were completely drunk were allowed to squeeze in. Some nearly transparent from excessive rotgut consumption or shaking, dying-right-on-the spot winos were given quick access to their remedy.

"Just look at him! He might die in a few minutes. Father, come on in - and you over there, just shut up!"

After an emotional time spent in the vodka line, I returned to my colleagues carrying a mundane, clinking briefcase.

Security and disguise were practiced in Russia for a long time. Our revolutionary forefathers were especially good at such things. It was clear for any Russian with a sound mind what I was carrying in my clinking case around Lenin Time. But like in many other vital situations, everyone knew but didn't tell "them."

"They", or people ranked as authorities, drank like us anyway just in different places such as the Kremlin, the KGB headquarters, and the rosewood furnished Party offices. We suspected they didn't spend much time in vodka lines – a task assigned to small fries and demoted KGB agents.

On my return, my comrades had already prepared simple snacks they brought from their homes: bread, hard-boiled eggs, smoked sausage, cheese, green onions, radishes – all placed neatly on a fresh newspaper. A few heavy, not-exactly-transparent drinking glasses were ready as well. For lunch vodka, the measure was three quarters of a glass; in the case of a rotgut, the glass was full.

We drank standing in a circle, finishing our portions in a few gulps, exhaling noisily after downing it and chewing our sausage and onions that tasted so fine in the fresh air. Now it was time to share our troubles and joys, but after a glass of vodka all troubles seemed to be far away. The happy feeling of brotherhood condensed in our circle. At Lenin Time, the same feeling permeated factories and offices, secret labs and sport venues, police stations and collective farms all over our great socialist motherland.

We suspected our strategic nuclear forces were honoring Lenin Time as well. There was a special joke related to the possible complications from bunker drinking:

A furious general interrogates his defiantly speechless subordinates:

'I'm asking you for the last time – who pressed button number nine?'

And then after a minute of silence, the general concedes:

'Okay, you are dismissed. Fuck Holland!'

Our kind of humor. But then, in the winter of 1974, we served our vodka Mass with open hearts full of joy. We felt we could absorb the vibrant essence of being full of love and compassion.

In our circle, we enjoyed simple things on which our existence rested, smoothing our differences with the rough-tasting cheap vodka, sausage, and onions. We cherished our freedom from the rat race so common in democratic societies. We had our brotherhood and shared the sweet feeling of being from the underclass: working hard, although not on a regular basis.

Personally, I was incapable of performing any duties after the first glass of vodka. Normally, after a few spicy, but not cruel comments my colleges made about the frailty of intelligentsia, my already red-faced boss sent me home. Then, after an hour-long struggle with sleep in a subway car, I finally made it home, joining at last with my all-forgiving and always-waiting couch.

I always admired my well-trained virile comrades for being capable of work for a few more hours after we finished our vodka lunch.

Lenin Time was over and the rest of the day softly slipped into oblivion. My country was drunk and content again.

Postscript

Now a thought or two. Most of the soviet working men and women (gender equality was a success in this case) could get lost from their work place and get drunk anytime they wished. They always could find plenty of drinking buddies who were busy doing the same thing – getting lost and getting drunk during the work day. Just don't say it's healthier to spend eight hours in some assembly line or to perform some idiotic, boring, and depressing duties at some bank, office or a store five days a week.

Now consider free medicine, free universities and no unemployment. Then don't forget that we had cheap basic groceries, excellent public transportation, and affordable housing.

Which freedom do you prefer – freedom to do, or freedom not to do?

I'm going for both!

Soldier and Larissa

SOLDIER

"I just wanted to catch a cab, when suddenly – I don't really know why, the sidewalk I stood on tilted and that lamp-post crossed the street and jumped at me like crazy." From Soldier's late-night conversation with police officers on Gorky Street in downtown Moscow.

Soldier was a well-built, confident man with plenty of charisma. He had a strong chin, a tall forehead and clear blue eyes. He joined one of the first brigades of Moscow hippies where he acquired his noble rank. As a true veteran of the movement, Soldier did not give a shit about his space-time coordinates, most of the time being concerned only with acquiring any variety of alcohol or controlled substances. He could easily swallow the most disgusting alcohol beverage, a basic cough medication, a cheap Russian cologne, or Chanel #5 – almost anything that could deliver some buzz.

Soldier regularly pissed off parents of the girls he slept with by devastating their household stocks of liquor and wine. The disappearance of certain pills from medicine cabinets was usually discovered a few days later.

All that did not cause Soldier many problems because he had trouble remembering with whom he slept and when.

Soldier never stopped until he finished all available booze or buzz, and that sometimes caused him significant suffering. However, you would never see a tear in his eyes. His managed to stay calm most of the time. Soldier was tough and rarely lost his sharp sense of humor.

Now imagine some undisclosed location in Moscow. Soldier and Cohen are lying side by side on a bed in an agony of severe hangover. They stay motionless and speechless for a while.

Knowledgeable reader! If you are familiar with this circle of crime and punishment, you know how it feels: your heart pounds like a steam engine and misses some beats, your head is squeezed by a sadistic torture device, and your Great Inquisitor tightens its grip. You can't even think of the disgusting taste in your dry mouth. You feel you are near the end of your miserable existence. Suddenly, being overwhelmed by an unusual religious zeal, you beg your Maker to rescue you for the last time. You promise that you will quit drinking.

Similar thoughts probably were crossing my friends' minds when Soldier managed to whisper:

"Hey Cohen!

Cohen was only able to move his eyes in response. Soldier gathered all that was left in him and uttered clearly:

"One, two, three, you are dead!"

"You bastard!" Cohen responded.

They laughed coarsely, moaned, and laughed again.

Soldier had the spirit of a true entrepreneur. He worked for a while as a nurse in a psychiatric institution where he helped a few patients to return into the world, of course after they paid him a reasonable fee. He had the right key.

Soldier disregarded conventions and was not always up to etiquette.

One sunny afternoon a desperate comrade swallowed too many codeine pills, and in a minute spilled the content of his stomach on a dusty Moscow sidewalk. While the victim gasped, trying to recuperate from stress and frustration, Soldier didn't waste precious time. He combed through the steaming pile of vomit with a twig scrupulously digging for the valuable undigested pills.

Soldier wrote lyrics for pop tunes and considered himself a poet. One of these songs became a major hit, so he began collecting decent royalties. I don't think anybody heard anything poetic from Soldier after he scored the big one. Sometimes, when he suffered from hangover and had no cash left, he simply called the state agency collecting royalties, introduced himself and asked with royal simplicity:

"How much do I have now?"

It was always enough to stay drunk for a few more days.

Soldier had a unique way with words. He made major contributions to Moscow slang. Many people imitated his style of conversation and his unique intonation. Soldier could simply say: "I'll telephone you tomorrow morning," and it sounded like a line from Alexander Blok (a beloved Russian poet of the early 20th century) recited by a good actor.

At some point in his life, Soldier began addressing any man he telephoned as Nikolai and every woman as Leuba. Soon it became routine in our circle.

Later in his life, Soldier always lived with women who were grocery store clerks. He always had enough food and could get vodka on a whim.

Sometime in the past, Soldier had a charming wife and beautiful twin daughters. His former father-in-law's name was Ovid. Ovid was a member of the writers' union, had a nice *dacha* (summer home), access to a special, well-stocked grocery store, and some other useful privileges provided for legitimate Soviet writers.

Ovid was a paratrooper commando during World War II. He was decorated with the highest Soviet military award, the gold star of a hero of the U.S.S R. Ovid earned it by cutting the throats of dozens of sleeping German soldiers.

"A strange thing," Soldier commented with a shrug after telling this story.

Soldier didn't hurt his enemies, he only pissed them off. That could've been a decent epitaph, but against all odds, he did well for many years to come until finally a cancer killed him.

Even so, I still can see him clearly marching to the mystery of his future.

THE DANCE

I'd been hearing these stories about the Krestovik gang, annoying tales of the working-class suburbs. I was told if a gang member makes a move on a girl and this girl would dare to say no, she simply disappeared. The Krestoviks hung out at the major town's intersection, also known as the "Krest" or the cross. That's where their name came from.

Krestoviks always looked for someone to beat up: new kids on the block, Jews, hippies, homosexuals – whoever came first. I didn't worry about Krestoviks too much because at that time I was a singer in a rock band based in Lubertzi and we were quite popular among the locals.

I was fully immersed in the rock'n'roll craze of the early seventies. We rehearsed for hours, not even drinking until we were through. We played great stuff: Jimi Hendrix, Led Zeppelin, Santana, etc. We learned songs listening to the records we got on the black market. These records were hot commodities and sold for 50-60 rubles each – a third of an average monthly Soviet salary.

Every Friday and Saturday we played for dances at the Lubertzi Palace of Culture and were paid monthly 70 rubles each! It was incredible – we played rock'n'roll openly and got paid on a regular basis.

The colossal gray Palace of Culture had fat columns, a heavy portal adorned with the hammer-and-sickle insignia, a glamorous staircase and other attributes of a style of architecture we called "Classical Stalinism." The three-story marvel had an 800-seat concert hall that could be easily converted into a dance floor and plenty of room designated for various activities such as music and dance lessons, woodworking, sewing, writing workshops, etc.

Lubertzi was a gloomy, spooky-after-dark small town 20 or so miles from Moscow. Its dirty, narrow streets were lined with identical faceless five-floor apartment buildings. The yards were crisscrossed with endless clotheslines with drying sheets and underwear. Diligent *babushkas* (old women) wrapped in kerchiefs scanned every passerby with their piercing, inquisitive stares. Just walking past them was a dreadful experience.

Traveling to gigs together with Stepanyan, the band's fiery lead guitarist and a Jimi Hendrix fanatic, proved to be a wise decision. Once when we were riding a bus to the gig, a pig-faced thug approached us and said with a smirk:

"Boys, give me 44 kopecks."

The bus fell silent. Everybody knew it was a prelude to extortion of more money or a serious beating. Both Stepanyan and I wore shabby blue jeans, had long black hair and that infamous pensive look. My colleague was also equipped with a huge, beautifully curved nose.

It was clear: we were the only Jews and hippies on the bus, even though my colleague was an Armenian.

As we consolidated our ranks, the pig face unexpectedly laughed and pointed his fat finger at my comrade's pale face.

"I know you! You are Stepanyan, a great guitarist, and you" his finger now pointed at my face, "You are a new singer in the band."

We exhaled, feeling much better. The thug kept on blowing bubbles of idiotic laughter.

"It was a joke, boys! I don't need your 44 kopecks!"

His pig-face was friendly now.

Our new friend got off on the next stop. We looked at each other and shook our heads. This time rock'n'roll saved us from trouble. However, most of the time it caused us trouble.

The powerful trio I sang with – guitar, bass and drums – was a part of a big combo with an extended brass section. Every night the full band played two sets of jazz-rock instrumentals. Usually, after two sets the brass section got really exhausted from excessive drinking. It was natural because their drink of choice was pure alcohol mixed half-and-half with tap water. They always asked us to play whatever we wanted without them in the third, final set, and all we wanted was rock'n'roll!

We gave our music all we had and played it as loud as we could in front of a few hundred shaking and screaming fans. Fortunately, the Krestovik gang didn't mind our music and the progressive director of the facility chose not to pay attention to the politically incorrect rock'n'roll set.

I can proudly recall that I put on a strong performance on my first night. I jumped and shrieked on stage at my very best after drinking a good portion of the brass section's half-and-half bon voyage donated by my older band colleagues. We cranked up Led Zeppelin's "Immigrant Song" and after finishing the first verse I noticed that the people stopped dancing and stared at me with surprised looks on their faces.

The next night the dance attendance doubled. Everyone attributed this to my triumphant debut in the third set. I suspected that my success also had something to do with Led Zeppelin's genius, which had not been publicly exposed to Lubertzi's audiences before that momentous night. But happiness in this life rarely lasts too long – my quick fame was in shambles very soon.

The next Friday our brass section had drunk too much even by their own inscrutable standards.

During the first break the band leader, a trumpet player and a jazz survivor of the ancient Beat generation, stared at me intently after failing an attempt to get off a dusty old couch in the green room. His look was dull and unfocused, and his hand with a half empty glass was frozen in motion. He struggled to recover his speech facilities.

"Fuck it!" he uttered at last, giving up his attempts to become vertical. Suddenly he was overwhelmed with hiccups.

"Boys! I can't do it. *Hick.* Go and …*hick…* kick their asses. *Hick.*"

Stepanyan and I looked around. Other members of the brass section weren't in much better shape.

"Let's improvise!" Stepanyan said.

After hearing the word improvise, the band leader failed a last-ditch effort to stand up, belched and handed me his glass with "half-and half." I finished that sacrifice in one go.

A few minutes later we were on stage and I jumped, shook my hair and screamed with hair-raising intensity, "Woman, do you need louloulouaave?"

But it was not a beautiful woman who answered this call by jumping on stage, wringing her hands and squealing in ecstasy.

Oh no! It was a well-respected 72-year-old Jewish gentleman, the director of the facility. Under his leadership, the Palace of Culture was awarded a special red banner and honorable third place in the national competition for Palaces of Culture.

Now the director's reputation was ruined because that very night the District Young Communist Organization had sent a special delegation to the Palace to evaluate how well the facility was doing on the socialist culture front. And there I was, jumping and shaking my long hair on stage in the shabby blue jeans and screaming in English! I was an agent of the rotten capitalism!

The next day the director was on stage before the show.

"Get the fuck out of here!" the director shouted. He put his index finger in my face shaking, raging and cussing non-stop.

I was discharged dishonorably from the cultural frontier. The whole band including the brass section begged for clemency on my behalf, but the director was adamant:

"He must fuck off!"

That was all that my band mates heard from him ever since. The director was known as a very polite and restrained man, but he was cussing sporadically for weeks after my disastrous performance.

I was banished from the rock'n'roll paradise in Lubertzi, a wretched alien in the land of the victorious proletariat.

I learned more about aliens many years later, and thousands of miles away from Moscow. My American green card clearly stated that I was a *resident alien*, a term I thought belong to the world of science fiction. Anyone endowed with this title had to carry it like a snail shell - anywhere you flew or crawled.

But even though many years have passed, I still clearly remember that Friday night, just a day before my eviction from the Lubertzi's Palace of Culture.

I was on stage with my friends ready to start the show. Two exhilarating weeks I spent rehearsing and playing with the band passed as one day. It was a Friday night and the dance floor was filled with people – a good crowd!

But soon something strange began to happen. A muscular Krestovik climbed on stage in the middle of a song and asked the drummer if he could play drums for a while. The drummer let him do that immediately. The bastard proceeded to screw up the song we played and I was mad.

The other band members behaved as if nothing unusual had happened. The bass player moved close to me and whispered in my ear:

"Stay cool, keep on singing."

I took his advice - he was from Lubertzi.

Five minutes before, the dance floor was packed with frantically dancing people, but now it was empty: people cleared it and quietly huddled along the walls. Something else was happening: a dwarf named Kolya hobbled into the center of the room.

The next instruction came from Stepanyan:

"We have to play *Myasoedovskya Street* now. Don't ask why."

I knew the song, the criminal underworld favorite, an obligatory tune in the repertoire of every Soviet restaurant band.

I took a deep breath and we started the song.

In the middle of the dance floor, a large circle was forming. Kolya the dwarf was in the center of it. Tough looking athletic guys with low foreheads and short haircuts ran in a circle with their hands placed on each other's shoulders. The Rites of Power were in progress.

They ran faster and faster, a gray circle in the middle of the room decorated with plaster hammers and sickles and five pointed stars.

Kolya the dwarf swirled in the center of everything stretching his arms toward the ceiling, the triumphant and menacing King of the Dance.

We kept on playing.

God and Beloved

GOD LOVES SEX AND BOOKS

It was not too easy to eat *pelmeni* (Russian dumplings) without using hands, but I gave it a good try.

We dropped at this small corner *pelmennaya café* on a chilly November afternoon. A few bottles of cheap port clinked cheerfully in a tote bag, betraying our unlawful intentions.

It was a good place to have some inexpensive food and share the previous night's adventure stories. We settled at the back of the room and filled our glasses under the table, right by a faded sign on the wall that warned:

"To bring and to consume alcoholic beverages is strictly prohibited!"

Being a sophomore in college, I was already well acquainted with these forbidden pleasures. That afternoon for some unknown reason, I finished my port ration, put my hands behind my back and plunged without any hesitation into a plate full of hot, slippery *pelmeni* floating lazily in the melted butter and sour cream.

Under these circumstances I met God for the first time. He wore black pants and a black, medieval-looking hoody.

He had a goatee, long dark hair and a penetrating gaze. His intelligent eyes had a spark of madness.

God smiled and giggled softly as he cordially invited us to his home. On the topmost, fourteenth floor, he knocked at his door and then the first miracle happened.

The door was opened by an absolutely naked, except for glasses, brunette with beautiful curves. And she was friendly! She was God's soul mate, Beloved.

I loved everything in God's quarters! There were a few people I didn't know in the living room drinking and doing drugs, but I don't remember any other details from my first visit with God, even whether I got laid immediately upon my arrival or later. Alcohol and excitement obscured all memories, but for the magnificent entrance.

One thing was clear: God's dwelling was the most remarkable place I had entered since my puberty.

The Books

God owned his place, a one room apartment with a good-sized kitchen and a big balcony. At that time, he was the only person of our age I knew who owned an apartment. From the balcony, you could see the Kremlin's towers looming in the distance. God's neighborhood was quiet and green. It had a patch of single-family houses – very unusual for Moscow – called Falcon Village.

There were fences, gardens, and even some garages there. A permanently spaced-out comrade nick-named Gusak the Intelligentsia, a Falcon's resident, once told me that Falcon Village was the very first cooperative in post-revolutionary Moscow. According to Gusak, his grandfather, who worked in the KGB, paid for the house. The price of his home was the same as the price for a box of oranges. Falcon Village was a KGB settlement.

Later, the KGB had to make room for Soviet writers, so current residents belonged mostly to these two groups and were rather invisible behind their fences.

God's house was the only high-rise in the area. His apartment was a high school graduation gift from his father, who was a dean of visual arts in the famous Stroganov College of Art and Design. All of us lived with our parents at that time and had limited possibilities for parties and other debauchery, but God could do anything he wanted in the privacy of his own apartment. And everything was exactly what God dutifully did at his place.

After entering God's apartment, you immediately knew that you had made it to free territory. You had found a safe place after a long and treacherous flight from the be-a-good-kid land lined with transparent houses where plump mommies cooed heartily over their boiling vegetables and fat daddies with hairy hands scanned the environs with their lewd eyes.

You felt safe behind God's locked, shabby door and the drawn, heavy, black-and-red satin curtains dropping from the ceiling to the floor. It was a free zone where you could be what you were.

All of your petty vices and little dirty secrets itched to get into the open under the tolerant light of multicolored lamps hidden in unexpected places – under the table, among the countless books, and in the corner behind a huge linen chest. God had a remote control for the lights by his bed – an enormous mattress laying on the floor. The mattress was surrounded on three sides by God-made, crude, wooden bookshelves.

Bookshelves took almost all wall space in the room. They held amazing books – 19th Century first editions of Russian philosophers, rarities of poetry, history, fiction and art. At God's place, I read my first Chinese poem and got acquainted with Schnitzler, Borges and Huysmans. Science fiction, fairy tales, children's stories, and literary criticism were also well-represented in God's Library.

I didn't see a single trashy book on God's bookshelves. Like most thing about him, God had an unusual and very specific taste in books: he loved gothic fairy tales and insane artist's prose, such as Munch's "Alpha and Omega," or "The Other Side" by Alfred Kubin.

In our life, books were valuable and hard-to-obtain commodities. Every book in bookstores was supposed to strike a chord with the proletariat.

The way to verify a book's ideological validity was very simple: one just had to ask, "Can the proletariat gain anything by reading this particular book?"

Somehow, our proletariat had nothing to gain by reading Pasternak, Akhmatova, Nabokov, Berdyaev, Sartre, and many other noteworthy authors. Most of the books that interested us were limited editions and were impossible to find among official writers' dreadful output, volumes of Lenin and Marx, and countless brochures with Brezhnev's speeches.

Nevertheless, God managed to get most of the books he wanted and he spent most of his limited resources buying them. He used catalogs and knew some antiquarian booksellers and black market dealers. For the love of books, God was ready to go far.

One summer, a young French scholar, an expert in Russian avant-garde poetry who happened to be gay, became a regular at God' place. He was impressed with my friend, his life style and his environment. Being a polite and considerate visitor, the Frenchman bought wonderful books for God in the *Beriozka,* a special hard currency store for foreigners only.

Thankful God asked me: "Do you think I have to screw him for the books?" I suggested to introduce the Slavicist to our local gay, Pavlik, make them both drunk and turn off the lights. It worked, and a relieved God remained what he was: straight and polygamous.

Sex

Another of God's passions was sex itself, to which he was as much devoted as to the books. There was a large mirror installed above his love altar. God's mattress could, and did, serve six to seven people at once. If mirrors could speak, the one above the mattress would have many fascinating stories to tell. Everything I could imagine about sexual intercourse occurred on this holy ground.

Pleasant surprises were saved for new guests and friends of the house. I was lucky to become friends with God and Beloved almost immediately after our first meeting and did enjoy my privileges.

I can't forget the massage given to me by two traveling lesbians. A delightful couple, they settled at God's place for a few weeks during which he persistently and unsuccessfully tried to change their sexual habits.

Oral sex thrived in God's territory. I cannot count all the terrific blowjobs I was blessed with in the friendly atmosphere of his home. That's where I also received my baptism into group sex.

There were often two women in God's bed, but only one of them, Beloved, was always the same.

God and Beloved were together since the age of sixteen, but neither of them wanted to vulgarize their relationship with marriage. Other live-in women were replaceable. There were accepted as one of the trio for purposes of sex and enlightening education.

God could proclaim on a whim, "I want a new fuck!" and faithful Beloved put on her coat and ventured into the frigid Moscow winter night to find a woman for him – something that many men can't even dream about.

In his turn, loving God always helped Beloved find a new lover for herself. Beloved never hesitated to engage in sex with any man or woman she liked.

If a new woman stayed longer than a week, she was considered a wife. The only problem with wives was that they all went nuts after a short while. Perhaps they couldn't withstand the intensity of sex and education.

The most resilient and long-lasting wife, the prettiest of them all, was Favorite. God actually married her officially. A charming red head, Favorite radiated hormones with such strength that it was impossible not to have an erection as soon as you glimpsed her - even remembering her… She was the queen of love in God's land for two years.

One summer, God, Beloved, and Favorite traveled together to Gourzouf, a small resort town by the Black Sea.

A notorious, subtropical paradise, Gourzouf was loved for its beaches, clear sea, abundance of beer and wine, and really loose morality among vacationers. But even in that place where many people looked loose and eccentric, God's trio appeared different and drew a lot of attention.

In Gourzouf, God wore a summer version of his black Gothic clothing, and his two women were wrapped in a Sari-like colorful fabric exposing their tight butts and barely covering their glamorous breasts. The three of them were always together, slowly parading the dusty streets of an old town in the midst of an admiring and envious public.

However, my friends had trouble finding a place to rent. The only accommodations in town were rooms rented in private homes. After seeing God and the women, inquisitive owners tried to figure out their relationship. God hated their curiosity, but eventually had to deal with it, introducing Favorite as his wife and Beloved as her sister. It was difficult for him because God normally never lied.

The trio spend three days in peace before my irresponsible drunken behavior messed up everything.

I bumped into the God trio at a beer stand by a bus station. There were hugs, laughter and excitement, especially on my part. We bought plenty of wine and food, and headed to my friends' newly acquired residence. As always, I had a great time with God. We were getting drunk quickly and were carelessly unaware that the window in the room where we partied was open. Light calico curtains flowing in the sea breeze gave the sneaky house owner a good opportunity to watch the pleasant sight of a wife passionately giving head to a family friend while the husband and the wife's sister peacefully discussed some obscure book while seated on a coach nearby. The next morning my friends were mercilessly evicted from their abode.

After one year of living together, God and Favorite got officially married. Soon after that, some theosophical dudes lured Favorite into their web of Tantrism mixed with Russian orthodox mysticism. She began to disappear, sometimes for weeks. She also became mentally challenged. As she was getting crazier and crazier, God had to take extreme measures. He banished theosophy on his territory, kicked out all mystic bastards, and checked Favorite into a psychiatric institution. The latter was a very hard decision for him to make. I couldn't even imagine him walking voluntarily into a facility because he was legally mad and our psychiatric Gestapo could lay their hands on him anytime.

Favorite got better and God was ready to take her home before Christmas when the last straw was suddenly broken. One of the mystic dudes managed to get in to see her with a huge bouquet of red roses. He showed up barefoot, wrapped in a white sheet and wore a white turban. The son-of-a-bitch delivered a message to Favorite: the heavenly groom she was expecting was going to take her on Christmas night.

After such great news, Favorite went nuts completely and for good. During the next few years, she dropped by God's place from time to time and stayed a day or two. She didn't talk – only giggled.

Once Favorite showed up with a photograph of a Rasputin-like old man with a very long beard. It was the elder Porphyry, famous for his radical treatment of all physical and spiritual maladies. His method was simple: you lay on a bench naked while Porphyry said a prayer. After that, his assistant threw a large bucket of ice-cold water on you and you were good to go.

Somehow, the elder acquired a significant and predominantly female following. Favorite hung about the elder for a while and then disappeared into the wilderness completely.

The last time I saw Favorite at God's place, she was a shadow of herself, emaciated and still giggling without saying a word.

"Don't even think of it," God said with a sad frown on his face. "She has gonorrhea and no brain."

Freedom in the Interior

Nobody was forced to do or not do anything in God's place. Most visitors felt very comfortable in the free territory. Of course, it could look weird for a newcomer: somebody could sit on the floor rocking quietly, a philosophical discussion would be heating up in one corner while a jovial copulation was in progress in another. Anybody could peacefully raise a glass of vodka, roll a joint or load a syringe.

There were no substances prohibited in God's home, so you could abuse yourself in any possible fashion. All gifts of booze and dope were accepted with gratitude and split evenly among all who craved it. Food, both physical and spiritual, and bodies were generously shared.

There was a lot to look at in God's home. One wall in the living room was covered entirely with an immense collage. You could study it for hours – there were Bosch reproductions, Che Guevara, Dali, naked Beloved and wives, young Lenin, hippies in California, the rainbow-shrouded *Kosmokrator*, and a bunch of other peculiar images.

The kitchen door was clad in gleaming copper. There was a God-made ceramic ashtray on a kitchen table in the form of an arching naked woman with her legs spread. You had to stick your cigarette between her legs to shake of the ashes.

God was a hard-core pacifist and normally didn't used violence for any reason, though he was stocky and strong. Only once did I see God get physical. He grabbed one defiant guest by the shoulders, lifted him in the air, and bellowed: "Are you saying I am not a pacifist?"

The house cat, Cincinnatus, was quite a character. An elegant black creature, he was named after the main character from Nabokov's *Invitation to a Beheading*. God swore that the cat always watched him when he typed or made love.

Once I saw Cincinnatus push a stack of books from the shelf onto someone he didn't like.

One day, God let him outside and Cincinnatus disappeared. After that, some people claimed they saw him running around with a horde of female cats.

God Withstands Changes at the End of the Twentieth Century

After a while, God quit his library job he had for many years in the Academy of Science and devoted himself entirely to books and sex while Beloved successfully supported their household. For a long time, she worked as a nude model, but God and Beloved had a strategic plan for their life they kept secret. One day, surprising everybody, Beloved enrolled in the Stroganov College of Art and Design. She studied jewelry for four years.

Now it was God's turn to make money and he took a job as a night watchman. Two years after her enrollment, Beloved managed to begin producing jewelry for sale. She made silver earrings shaped like cut-off human feet and arms, dragon necklaces, and other odd jewelry. God helped her to cut stones and polish metals. They made decent money, bought more books and ate well. They were happy.

God always had "no admission" periods when he opened his door to no one. He rarely answered the telephone and didn't have a door bell. Actually, he had a door light, a small red electric bulb that flashed when someone pushed the button on the door. But the bulb was usually lost somewhere among books. You could press the button or knock at the door as long as you wished to no avail, so one could not tell what was happening behind God's door.

Gradually, "no admission" periods became more frequent – apparently something unusual was happening at God's place. And then the great news came: Beloved had given birth to a child – a son!

According to God's plan and precise astronomical calculations, the baby was conceived at a certain year, day and hour corresponding to a specific star's alignment. The boy was given the astrologically proven name of Gedaliah. He slept in a cradle God made himself. The cradle was decorated with 12 signs of the Zodiac and quotes from Li Po in Chinese.

After the baby was born, the live-in wives vanished and my friends became a more conventional family focused on rearing their first-born child.

Soon, Gedaliah became a lovely, robust little boy with dark, shining, clever eyes. He learned fast: at the age of five, he could read and write. He also knew some English and German words because Beloved spoke English and God knew German.

God had an extended collection of wonderful children's books from all over the world; he was well prepared a long time before his son's arrival. God and Beloved spent a lot of time with Gedaliah, teaching him everything they knew. They never sent him to school.

God didn't hide anything from his son and answered all of his questions, so Gedaliah learned many useful things pretty early. In particular, he knew exactly where babies came from and what to do if you want to have one.

One evening, according to the ritual, I brought my new date to God's home. Little Gedaliah was smitten by this cute, petite brunette and didn't waste any precious time. He grabbed her leg and began humping it. My date was shocked and embarrassed, but Gedaliah's parents were delighted and smiled approvingly. They liked her too. The little guy was only five years old, but already dug the main thing in life.

My last meeting with my friends in 1991 was sad. They talked about some dark, democratic forces threatening their lives, and had been demonstrating with communists on Red Square. They wanted the USSR to be restored. God proudly showed me a photograph in the Young Communist newspaper showing seven-year-old Gedaliah waving a big, red flag next to Lenin's Tomb.

God and Beloved didn't like capitalism or a money-oriented society. Old friends who hung out with democrats were banished. I was glad our ties were strong enough that they opened their door for me, even though they knew I lived in the most capitalist country in the world.

They were relieved to know that I was not fond of the Surplus Value religion. God told me that they were considering applying for political asylum in China, one of the last communist counties left on Earth.

Our goodbye was somber; sadness and anxiety filled our hearts.

Now, many years later, I call God on the telephone from time to time. Nobody answers – maybe it's one more blackout.

God moves in mysterious ways!

Kolya and Misha

COHEN'S ARREST

The hangover was severe, but we couldn't help laughing just looking at each other: two lanky, unshaved veterans of the movement with long, tousled hair and sardonic smiles, we were inflating endlessly stupid balloons. Flies died from our morning breath, but this time our precious exhalations were encapsulated into cheerful, multicolored, rubber bubbles. The balloons were supposed to entertain little children during their field trip to Izmaylovsky Park of Culture and Leisure.

Kolya Cohen was a park discotheque employee, but he was obliged to substitute for his irresponsible colleagues who didn't show up at work for various reasons. They could've still been unconscious after the previous night's drinking activities or fallen victim to the police's never-ceasing efforts to apprehend as many publicly intoxicated citizens as they possibly could.

That morning we were carrying our crosses together. Missing – with customary impunity – from my unobtrusive engineering duties, I was helping my friend to survive two very unpleasant hours until 11 a.m. when the beer kiosks in the park began to provide the long-awaited relief for the thirsty citizens.

The park was a perfect microcosm of our society, a preposterous facility, a welcoming refuge for the drinking population. The park also provided ceaseless entertainment for any reasonable observer.

An incredible absurdity of our Socialist motherland was exemplified in the park at an almost mythological level.

Most of jobs in the park were ridiculous and very entertaining, plus each employee had plenty of free time – enough to live their lives to the fullest.

A few of our comrades joined the motley collection of park employees. Dar was a messenger who normally had no messages to deliver. However, when some urgent errands were assigned to him by the suddenly-materialized-from-nothingness park authorities, diligent Dar disappeared sometimes for a few days trying to find the most efficient way to fulfill his duties.

Valichev was in charge of servicing billboards and posting numerous notices produced by the park's office. He successfully failed both of his duties.

But it was Kolya who became the first pioneer and explorer of the park employment after he was fired from all other jobs –normally, for excessive drinking at work leading to shamelessness and chronic arrests by the drunk squads.

To arrest drunks in public places was the major task assigned to the Soviet police. And, gosh, our cops were busy!

Some of them were scavengers picking up unconscious bodies from sidewalks, park benches, trains, buses and subway floors. That type of police activity was as common in Russia as the sight of a state trooper issuing a motorist a speeding ticket in the USA. Perhaps being picked up by a Drunk Squad was our Russian version of getting a speeding ticket. Most of us didn't have cars – they were too expensive to buy, and public transportation was good and cheap: for five kopecks you could ride a bus or the subway. A trolleybus ticket was four kopecks, and a street car ride, three kopecks.

However, we had serious speeding problems: drinking too much and too fast. So, when two vigorous Russian cops were peeling off someone's limp, helpless body glued to the pavement with dried vomit, a passerby could have the same thought as an American motorist passing someone else's stopped car:

"Not me this time, pigs!"

Police vans used by the Drunk Squads to collect their prey were called *Lunohods* (Moonwalkers). I saw one them passing the park's office where we were still engaged in the balloon enterprise. We still had one hour until the beer kiosks opened.

I felt desperate enough to ask Kolya about his experience with Drunk Squads – he had a formidable expertise in this matter.

"Do you really want to know it," he asked me with a wry smile.

"Sure," I responded.

Kolya paused for a minute or so and began telling his sad story.

"When they pick you up and charge with 'an appearance insulting human dignity' (an official definition describing a person being obnoxiously drunk), you will be transported to a *vitrezvitel*, a sobering up facility run by police. There, you will be stripped of your clothes and shoved in an ice-cold shower. After that, you will be tied to a bed – still naked – in a big, ugly room together with twenty or so suffering comrades. They will let you go the next morning with a bill for the services delivered.

And finally – it's the worst part – an official paper will be mailed to your work place. Normally, you get fired if your boss receives two such papers in one year.

My boss told me he received two *vitrezvitel* papers with my name on it last week. That's why we are doing balloons," Kolya grinned and began inflating a red balloon. We both giggled.

Two *vitrezvitel* papers in one week was well beyond anything conceivable.

However, nothing could threaten Kolya's job security because we didn't have unemployment in my country. You had to have a job if you were older than eighteen or after you were graduated from a college. All fellow citizens had to work for the purpose of keeping our motherland prosperous and powerful. If you didn't work for more than three months, you would be labeled as a *tuneyadtetz* (parasite) and expelled from Moscow. In that case, you were allowed to settle not closer than 100 kilometers from Moscow. But life in Moscow was much better than life anywhere else – more food in grocery stores, more job opportunities, and more fun.

Once you had been expelled from Moscow, it was very difficult to come back legally, because you were missing that magical stamp in your passport (the only one legal I.D. in Russia at that time) that allowed you to live and to work in the city. That stamp was called *propiska* and was the major feature of a handy system created by Stalin to control potentially troublesome citizens.

Before the expulsion, repeat offenders, notorious drunks, dissidents, and other scum were given a chance to prove themselves worthy of our socialist society. They were assigned mandatory jobs at assembly lines, grocery stores, and yes – at city parks, the lowest paying jobs.

Kolya could not be expelled further than Izmaylovsky Park. That was it, the very bottom of the glorious Socialist Heaven. So naturally being untouchable, he enjoyed his loose work schedule and wild drinking in the park. It really didn't matter how often the Drunk Squads arrested him.

Kolya somehow managed not to be arrested in the park, though cops once chased him all the way to a locale where they all almost died from laughter after being stuck in the mud together.

Once when Kolya was late for his discotheque uploading duties, he arrived in a cab driving into the center of a dance floor. The dancers scattered and Kolya dropped out of the car and crawled to the stage, cursing everything on earth.

But all these park pranks were just a small part of adventures we shared.

Fly Easy

One day Kolya and I brought two bottles of champagne into the peaceful cafeteria on the second floor of a large dietary grocery store in downtown. We asked a cheerful, ruby-cheeked clerk to give us drinking glasses, and we filled one of them for her. She accepted the gift smiling and we proceeded with our champagne lunch at a table, ignoring the slightly shocked audience. Russian winos normally don't frequent dietary facilities in their eternal search for drinking glasses.

I remember that one clear, cold, December night when we drank champagne again. We walked down a snowy street in downtown by the House of Actors, just one block from KGB headquarters. We offered a drink to every passerby.

"Happy New Year!" we shouted, handing a bottle to laughing girls with sparkling cold eyes and long, dark hair flowing down their soft, silver fur coats. In the blurry street, snowflakes danced under the dim, yellow street lights.

Time had slipped away painlessly, and now we walked in dormant, solitary streets on a serene summer night. The air was cool, restless and full of dreams.

We walked for hours, talking about anything but time – an intoxicating sermon of freedom and carelessness warmed by a refined sensation of a friend's shoulder being so close.

A cold, amber drink spurted from a snorting vending machine. A red sign "Cream Soda" gleamed in the dark. It always tasted so good after midnight.

Sometimes we met another band of nightwalkers walking towards us. We stopped for a minute, lit our cigarettes and nodded to each other. There was no need to talk – we belonged to the same clergy.

We proceeded with our journeys without looking back, dissolving soon in the whispering flow of wind, trees, and blurry street lights. The moonlight outlined the dark silhouettes of our beloved city. It was a young night in June…

Leningrad Syndrome

Kolya's Leningrad Syndrome developed when his photo still adorned a special display in the lobby of the Hydro Project skyscraper. Big red letters on top of the display stated something unthinkable: Kolya was one of the best employees, a winner of the Socialist Completion for the "Hydro Project" workers. Kolya had a M.A. in mine engineering and had done something useful in this formidable institution. I still don't understand how it could be possible, but one thing was clear: Kolya was an engineer at that time like all mortals.

The Hydro Project building dominated the skyline of the northern part of Moscow and was famous for the largest Lenin's-head display in the city. It was almost 60 feet from our founder's bald patch to his goatee. The immense red banner with Lenin's head was hanging from the roof of the skyscraper on all major holidays. It covered fifteen floors and you could enjoy it from miles away.

The Hydro Project was located on Leningradsky Avenue, an attractive straight and wide street that became Leningradsky Highway outside of the city. It started at the Red Square as Gorky Street and went all the way to Leningrad, a sweet destination about 400 miles from Moscow.

Everything was different and tempting in Leningrad. Plenty of beer kiosks opened at 8 a.m., so after warming up with a beer, you could stop at a nearby friendly *Rewmochmaya* (shot glass shop) and have a shot of vodka and a herring sandwich. After that, you could enjoy the Northern Venice in a good spirit walking down its beautiful straight avenues with a sufficient booze supply in your shoulder bag. Life was good in Leningrad!

Leningrad girls could cry real tears seeing you off on a train station, even though they had met you for the first time just a few days before at some obscure party. They were nice to you even when you had successfully passed out at a party and you had introduced yourself properly only when you woke up the next morning in the same bed with one of these lovely girls.

Leningrad also had an excellent reputation for its well-educated bouncers. One of these gentlemen was helping us out from a pub on Nevsky Prospect (a major, famous thoroughfare). After observing Kolya's substantial noble Jewish nose, the bouncer made a courteous comment: "Young man, you resemble Gogol!" The author of one of the greatest Russian novels, *Dead Souls*, was also an ardent anti-Semite. Kolya immediately awarded the enlightened bouncer a generous three-ruble tip.

Leningrad was the city of dreams and well worth a decent syndrome.

It all started on a regular Friday night in the summer of 1976 when Kolya said to his wife, "I am going to get cigarettes by the Sokol subway station. I'll be back in 20 minutes."

Then he disappeared into the wilderness.

On Sunday morning, his anxious wife got a long-distance call: "I am in Leningrad. I will be back tomorrow morning."

It was the beginning of the syndrome. After a while, it became Kolya's official diagnosis.

"I really don't know, doctor! It happens to me involuntarily. I began drinking with a bunch of friends. We began hopping from one pub to another in the morning, but when I got out of the last one in the evening, it was dark already. And then I saw this street sign: Nevsky Prospect. I was in Leningrad! How did I get there? I remember nothing, doctor!"

It was all written in the Kolya's case file. The Leningrad Syndrome became his official psychiatric diagnosis. Psychiatric care was the major escape route if you didn't want to be conscripted. Everybody dodging the draft on a cuckoo-basis was given the same diagnosis: 4-B, or schizophrenia in his own creative way:

God claimed he couldn't touch or look at any official paper and was incapable of opening the apartment's door and answering his telephone.

Dar was not aware of his name, address or gender.

Osheinikov marched around his apartment building wearing a brim of a lady's green velvet hat and singing environmental songs.

I could smell dead bodies in the public transport.

Soldier gave this statement at a police station:

"I was on the roof of Bolshoi Theater straddling these horses because I just wanted to enjoy –from the panorama of our beautiful city!" That was what our friend Shilov wrote at the police station explaining why he ended on the theater's roof where he attempted to climb on top of the world-famous, four-in-hand, bronze horses.

It proved to be sufficient for his diagnosis.

Kolya had his delightful Leningrad Syndrome for that purpose, and his condition seemed to be contagious, but still I managed to escape the full-fledged infection.

One day we decided to go to a bathhouse first thing in the morning. It was a useful thing to do if you were drinking for a week, a survival technique because you often could buy some beer there before any beer kiosks or liquor departments open.

On that morning, still drunk from the night before, we couldn't remember which day of the week it was, but we didn't forget to bring to the bathhouse a few bottles of vodka, dark rye bread, and some cheese and sausage. Our prospects for the day looked splendid. Everyone was full of enthusiasm.

However, when we arrived at our destination, right in front of the bathhouse doors, I suddenly stopped, feeling almost sober.

"Guys, I think today is my payday. I need to go to get more rubles! Bye!"

I was wrong, big time! As I pushed up the stairs to the third floor where the office of my company was located, I was stopped by my team-leader.

"Nikolai, where are you going?"

I trusted my instinct: today was not a payday!

"I just have to pick up some hoses for our equipment," I replied trying not to exhale in the direction of my boss and feeling smart.

"Get the fuck out of here, right away!" bellowed my commander and savior. In a few moments, stumbling and spreading alcohol fumes all around, I was running down the stairs. Luckily, no other boss saw or smelled me.

I escaped big trouble, but alas – I missed a possible trip to Leningrad. My Leningrad Syndrome didn't materialize.

Kolya and friends, whom I had left so abruptly in the bathhouse, did manage to reach their destination. Perhaps, it was a new manifestation of a phenomena described in physics as "tunnel effect," or maybe it was just a black-out lasting six hours enhanced by extensive drinking on the express train Aurora. Who knows?

After figuring out that he was in Leningrad, a puzzled Kolya annoyed the peaceful Leningrad pedestrians with an apparently bizarre question: "Excuse me! Tell me what the hell happened to Moscow? Where is it? What have you done to my city?"

Probably he looked frightening to the passerby – popped up piercing eyes, a wild pile of long, curly dark hair flying in the northern wind, a formidable eagle nose, and long, swift hands.

One-legged Submarine Captain, Frank Zappa's Vestige and No Fear

It was never boring to be in Kolya's company. He exuded charisma and confidence and had a unique, creative approach to whatever was happening in his proximity. Kolya was tall and slender, and was quite popular with women, so getting laid never was a problem for him.

But there was one particular trait of Kolya's that I admired the most: for all practical purposes, he was deprived of a sense of fear.

One morning, suffering from a particularly nasty hangover, shaking Kolya was heading to a cigarette kiosk not too far from his home when two policemen approached him with an apparent bad intent. After their first attempt to stop my friend, they were called "fucking goats." It was a deadly insult in the Russian underworld, often uttered after mentioning prison guards or police. Any decent cop was supposed to smash anybody using this word with his baton and possibly performing some footwork on a prostrated body at a police station afterwards.

But amazingly, that time after staring for a few moments at Kolya's outrageous foggy eyes, the policemen decided to use a format of verbal discussion:

"We are not!"

"Yes, you are!"

"This is not us!"

They went on like this for a few minutes. Of course, they arrested Kolya after all, proving one more time: they were fucking goats! However, the cops didn't touch a hair on Kolya's crazy head. They shared some beer with him in their *Lunohod* and he was released the next morning.

Kolya could defend himself pretty efficiently. If anybody called him a kike or just gave him a dirty look, a quick question followed: "Do you want to get it in your snout?"

If the question was not answered in 30 seconds or so, a quick punch arrived exactly at the mentioned location.

Kolya was very good with words and rarely missed a chance to demonstrate his reverence for the mighty Russian language:

"So you don't want to hear the word 'fuck'?"

"Are you sure you resent people who say 'fucking dick'?"

And so on…

It was a normal way for Kolya to get back at someone who disapproved of the use of foul language.

Kolya could really coin a phrase. Once I called him from New York and asked how things in Moscow were. He answered:

"We drink Absolut but puke the same."

You just started to drink with Kolya, and an adventure followed inevitably. That morning it was Kolya's turn to refund "dead soldiers." My parents were out of town for a week, and my friends had arrived at my place with girls and plenty of liquor and beer – as usual, a few hours after I waved goodbye to my folks.

Loaded with two heavy jingling bags, Kolya took off in the direction of a local liquor store where, according to recent rumors, he could refund empty bottles accumulated during the first two days of the festivities…

He came back the next day very drunk and happy without any booze or money.

"Oh man!" Kolya exclaimed, "I met this one-legged submarine captain yesterday afternoon in a vodka line. He lives near the liquor store where he is a regular. We went to his place to pick up a drinking glass. There was no furniture in his apartment except a few cardboard boxes and – it's a kick! – a cafeteria table missing one leg with a few dirty, cracked dishes on top of it.

"He told me he was a submarine captain during World War II, blasting German ships to pieces, and lost his leg in a battle. I think this duffer probably screwed up his leg after he was hit by a car while drunk.

"I would've had been back home yesterday noon if not for this wedding party I came across on the way back from the captain's quarters. I ended right in the middle of a wedding crowd; you know – all these drunk people wearing white shirts and ties, jammed in front of a doorway – the newlyweds, champagne, vodka, and accordion music. I think I danced with the bride – you know the way it normally goes – I got into a fight first, then we swore to love and to respect each other for ever, then fought again, etc...."

When we met in the summer of 1970, Kolya was notorious as a black market rock'n'roll dealer. He was buying forbidden records you couldn't buy in any official store, getting them from smugglers, and then copying and reselling this fabulous music. Just for a meager two rubbles, he could copy on tape practically any requested masterpiece. The volume of music passing through his hands was unbelievable: sometimes he handled 20-25 records per day. Kolya was a real expert in his business. He had excellent taste and knew English better than any of us.

It was Kolya who introduced me to Bob Dylan and Frank Zappa, whom I have admired ever since.

There was an eerie resemblance between Frank and Kolya in both appearance and spirit. Their profiles were equally inspiring, they both were provoking and outrageous.

Later, Kolya translated practically all Zappa's lyrics. Two kindred souls met at last.

The seventies were intense years marked by comradery and excitement. We cranked up Jimi Hendrix, Led Zeppelin, Santana, King Crimson, Pink Floyd and many others; we got drunk and stoned on a regular basis; and we practiced free love with our sisters-in-arms.

None of us gave a shit for our progressive socialist society or any other dogmas. I met Kolya practically every day. Eventually, we became "blood brothers," after sleeping together with a girl that was known as "Poker."

Poker was a frequent visitor at Kolya's place. She worked at a fashion agency and was tall, pretty, elegant and remarkably friendly. If she found you interesting enough, you could get in bed with her in a really expeditious manner, skipping most of the beaten-up dating rituals with blissful ease.

Fly Easy: Part 2

Two tall long-haired young guys are heading to a solitary park bench. Apparently, they have a few bottles clinking in a denim shoulder bag one of them carries. If you are experienced, you know they have some cheap port. The time is half past five. These two guys are Kolya and me. We already passed our beer phase. The summer is in full bloom. Old, noble lindens spread their mighty branches from both sides of a boulevard, swaying in a light afternoon breeze. The air is full of bird calls, sounds of city buses and children's voices.

We are walking down the Boulevard Circle (a chain of boulevards in downtown Moscow) taking our sweet time. From time to time, we harbor on secluded park benches to take a few sips from a disguised bottle. We look around carefully before getting to our port. Outdoor drinking is illegal, but such a sweet thing to do on a glorious August afternoon in the good, old city of Moscow. Our conversation is free flowing and meaningless. We are already quite drunk when Kolya makes a logical proposal:

"Let's polish it with some liquor."

We get a bottle of Chartreuse in the near-by liquor store, but it's hard to drink from the bottle – it is too thick and sweet.

I suggest we pay a visit to my friend Stepanyan who plays tonight with his band in the restaurant Moscow. It seems to be an appropriate place to finish our liqueur.

The restaurant is situated on the second floor of the monstrous Hotel Moscow, right across from the entrance to the Red Square. This ugly, imposing building was a jewel of Classical Stalinism, the dominant style of Moscow architecture during the Stalin's reign.

Ruby-cheeked collective farm girls with big boobs embracing all sorts of fruit and vegetables were painted on the walls in bright colors. Rachitic Dorian columns held a high ceiling where great fireworks were depicted against the dark skies adorned with five-point Kremlin stars.

The place was usually frequented by black marketers, provincial tourists, and representatives from various soviet legislative bodies who assembled in Moscow for one of their ceremonial votes. At every vote, our lawmakers rushed to raise their right hands as high as possible; didn't matter what they were voting for.

"Stepanyan" – the name I utter at the hotel entrance – tames for a minute a fearsome uniformed doorman, so we are able to squeeze in without paying a customary bribe.

Stepanyan waved us to the stage and immediately we were escorted by a hostess to a special table by the stage marked by a sign: "No Service."

A friendly waitress removes the sign and takes our order: a grilled halibut with roasted potatoes and Olivier salad. My favorite – grilled sturgeon – is too expensive. We sip our Chartreuse peacefully for some time when our server shows up with a cart carrying our order and one placed by Soviet deputies sitting at the next table. They had ordered a grilled sturgeon, but the fish on their plates looks just like our halibut. The waitress winked at us. We laugh and take another sip of liqueur.

Suddenly, two waitresses I haven't seen before show up.

"Sorry, boys! We need this table!" They grab the table and disappear in the dancing crowd.

We are sitting on two lonely chairs like two islands, still passing to each other our green bottle and sipping Chartreuse, surrounded by a dancing crowd. A few couples dance their way between us. We pass our bottle and drink more, laughing.

Then I remember nothing.

Always Prepared

Most of my friends dropped out from the Soviet System for good. It seemed a natural thing to do in the seventies. Conforming to our society was a dreadful thing to do, anyway.

However, we all, from the gentle age of eight, had a pin with a picture of baby Lenin attached to our gray school uniform. We were taught to love our common grandfather Lenin – he was such a lovable wise man.

In our textbooks, we saw a photo of smiling Vladimir Ilyich sitting on a park bench in a comfortable white suit and with his trademark *kepi*, surrounded by happy, laughing children. I was nine years old then.

Two year later we were awarded red silk neck scarfs at the Red Square right across from the Holy Shrine of the Mummy, the dark granite Lenin Tomb. We became young pioneers at the end of April, close to Lenin's birthday. We marched in orderly ranks feeling proud and excited. We belonged to the Movement! We raised our right hands saluting our socialist motherland:

"Young pioneers! You will fight for the victory of the communist party, be prepared!"

A formation of boys and girls with shining eyes in white shirts and red neck scarves flying in the fresh spring wing breathed out in unison:

"Always prepared!"

Down and Forward

My first entrance into Koyla's world was remarkably memorable. I got a full glass of port immediately after I cross the threshold of Kolya's apartment. Jimi Hendrix's "Voodoo Child" was cranked all the way up on his stereo. Everyone inside wore brand name blue jeans, worth 130 rubles on the black market (my engineer salary was 150 rubles a month), sat on the floor leaning against the wall, and had long hair and beards. Nobody spoke a word except for Shilov, who was sitting on the floor with his back against the wall. He struggled with severe hiccups and used any pause to say:

"Fuck the sister," or "I have a legitimate right!"

Drugs and booze were in abundance. All the King's men were happily drunk and stoned.

A great variety of bizarre and often obnoxious characters hung out around Kolya – Odessa, King of Sex, Duke, One-Handed, etc.… I always suspected it had something to do with the way Kolya spent his money. Money never stuck to him for long: didn't matter how much he got. Kolya was able to spend significant sums during just a few days. It was a party for everyone who happened to be in the neighborhood. The festivities lasted until everybody was broke and wasted.

Most of these jolly people crossed Kolya's orbit when he was at his drinking best. It was hard to escape his gravitational trap and the spontaneous time-lapses he triggered.

I remember an episode with a plumber who came to fix a faucet in Kolya's apartment and who ended staying and drinking with Kolya for two days. It was rather unusual for any member of the notorious tribe of Russian plumbers who were held in awe due to their incredible capacity to drink on the job. As a rule, any decent Russian plumber completely failed to fulfil his duties unless a customer offered him a glass of vodka, or at least put a glass of vodka in a prominent place, so he could observe it while working.

As time passed, the rock'n'roll records Kolya was dealing on the black market gradually were replaced by blue jeans, sneakers, boom boxes and other popular items smuggled from the rotten capitalist states. Kolya made more money, and being true to his impeccable reputation, spent everything promptly.

But the way he spent his money was quite different.

The Gnaw

If you wanted to get it, you had to go to one of the farmers markets where industrious collective *kolhozniki* (collective farm workers) and some city folk sold fresh produce and flowers they harvested in their small private gardens. You even could find meat there. The sellers came to Moscow from all 15 Soviet republics.

Big-nosed, mustached, swarthy, and proud merchants from the Caucasus lured customers with their sweet voices and exotic accents, waving their hairy hands above piles of fresh fruit and flowers. Laid back and mellow-talking Ukrainians offered apples, cherries, huge pumpkins, chunks of *salo* (cured pork fat) stuffed with garlic and jars of honey. Numerous Russian babushkas smiled kindly displaying potatoes, barrels of fermented cabbage and jars of pickles.

But you didn't need all this nice and expensive food. You looked for *kolhozniki* from Uzbekistan, the home of the best tomatoes, sweet onions, and grapes in the world.

And when you found these people, friendly people wearing their multicolor robes and skull caps, smiling behind piles of fragrant oval cantaloupes, honey-sweet watermelons and melt-in-your-mouth oblong "ladies' fingers" grapes, you simply asked:

"Do you have it?"

If you were lucky, after paying the price you received a small plastic bag of dried opium poppy ovaries.

At home with your curtains closed, you ground your catch in a coffee grinder, put a spoon or two of the powder into a cup and filled it with warm water.

Now you were ready to take "the gnaw."

The resulting mix tasted like stale straw. Consuming it was a nauseating process.

Once, during one of our long buzz-walks, we stopped for refueling at a secluded downtown yard. We ran out of water, but Kolya courageously swallowed two spoons of the ground poppy mix. He convulsed from disgust, brushed a few crumbs stuck in his mustache and pronounced:

"The Gnaw!"

In no time it became a brand name for the stuff among the involved Muscovites.

Soon, the gnaw became just one among many possibilities in Kolya's quest for drugs. He used everything he could get – barbiturates, codeine pills, synthetic and natural morphine stolen from hospitals and sold by some entrepreneurial nurses and doctors.

And then there was a thing called "blacky." In order to produce it, you took a fresh poppy flower, made a cut close in the stem, and squeezed the juice on a small mirror or a piece of glass. Then you cooked it with a cigarette lighter placed under the glass. After that, you diluted it in a spoon with water. Your blacky was ready for injection.

After having a shot, you faced two possibilities: you got high or you got 'shakers." The latter meant that every limb of your body, every hair on your head began to shake violently, sweat poured down your face, you heart tried to jump out of your chest and you gasped for air like a fish thrown on the sand.

I never took it, but every opportunity of getting it was worth a try for real dope cowboys. So special detachments armed with scissors and plastic were sent to collect any variety of poppies in city gardens.

Police responded, posting notices on railroad stations announcing:

"If you see a hairy youth inquiring about poppies grown in private gardens, inform the authorities immediately! These individuals are dangerous criminals!"

"Kolya, how can I tell a poppy from anything else in the dark?"

An angry whisper was uttered in response:

"Just shut up, turn on your back, and look at flowers against the moon!" from a scene at someone's *dacha* garden.

The substance Kolya used didn't change, but his dose went up. Some ugly characters now frequented his place. All they talked about was junk and what was standing in the way of getting it. After receiving a dose, any talk stopped, replaced with a contented, but short-lived, vegetative state.

A year later, there was no content or euphoria after injecting a dose, only suffering before getting it and then some rest; a twisted substitute of normality afterwards.

Crime and Punishment: Fall off the Wagon

The doorbell was ringing for a good twenty minutes when someone got off the chair and shuffled to the door and opened it. The rest of the crew kept on with their business at the kitchen table crammed with vodka bottles, glasses and dirty plates of food leftovers and cigarette butts. A rare vodka party – disrespected among junkies – was in full swing.

Then this official looking guy showed up in the kitchen and presented his police I.D., but still, none paid much attention to him. A couple of minutes later, Kolya looked at the newcomer and his I.D. and said handing a vodka glass to him:

"Hi, boss! Sit down and have a drink with us. You say neighbors called the police again? Yeah, that's what neighbors are for. I won't run away, you can arrest me later. Come on, here is your drink!"

Giggling Kolya poured a full glass of vodka, spilling it all over the table, stood up and handed it to the policeman, now spilling vodka on the floor.

I am not sure if it was Kolya's charisma or simply a pure Russian heart beating in the cop's breast, or if he just couldn't stand the sight of a full glass of vodka being senselessly spilled all over. Whatever it was, the glass was accepted.

The investigator spent the night at Kolya's place. He eventually passed out and slept on the same couch with Dar.

The next morning everybody was in shambles. After waking up, the investigator stared confusingly at the snoring Dar for some time. Groaning and moaning Kolya showed up in the kitchen looking for a cigarette. Then Kolya and the cop had more vodka.

"Listen, man," the policeman said, "I came here to investigate you. You have to go with me to the police station, or I will be in trouble! I can be fired, I have a family to feed, please!"

"You are a pig!" Kolya responded, "You are a fucking goat, but you are still more or less human. Let's go at once!"

Wobbling and stumbling, holding each other, they somehow made it to the police station. They straightened up and walked inside trying not to exhale. Being lucky, they reached the investigator's office without any trouble.

The investigator pulled Kolya's file out of his safe and threw it onto his desk. Then he looked at Kolya with suspicion and said:

"I am dying to take a leak. I'll be back in a minute. Stay here and don't touch anything on my desk!"

Grinning, Kolya barely waited until the investigator left the room. He grabbed his file, as well as a few more from the open safe, stuffed them under his thick sweater, and simply walked out of the police station. He safely returned to his home where the party was still in progress.

"Long live the liberation of the crooks!" he proclaimed joyfully. The files were torn to small pieces, burnt in the toilet bowl, and flushed.

Soon the investigator was knocking at Kolya's door. This time, the negotiations proceeded with a door chain locked.

"I trusted you, but you ruined my career. Give me my files back! I know the judge; we can shelve it all. Please, comrade Cohen!" the investigator blabbered. He began sobbing, but Kolya was relentless:

"Go to hell! I'm tired of you. Get lost! Fuck off!"

The next day an emergency meeting took place at the police station. After reviewing the investigator's report, a conclusion was made that Kolya was a shrewd and dangerous criminal, a local ringleader who has to be apprehended with minimal losses. An appropriate plan was set in motion by the drug squad.

A friend (in the junky world – someone who got high with you a few times) called Kolya in the morning:

"Listen, man! I got the shakes last night. I feel like I'm dying, no shit. Get me some fix, anything!"

They set up a meeting in half-an-hour at the entrance of the Sokol underground station nearby. That's where the narcs apprehended Kolya at the very moment he was passing that rat his remedy.

According to the same classic scenario, he was kept in a cell for two days – just long enough to be almost dead from the withdrawal. Then, shaking and exhausted, Kolya was dragged to an interrogation room. He sat on a chair in front of a desk with a bright lamp aimed at his inflamed eyes. A plain-clothed investigator was leaning back in his chair, a cigarette smoldering in his mouth.

"A full glass of the gnaw and a glass of water were sitting enticingly by the edge of the desk. The investigator stared at Kolya silently for a while and then uttered softly:

"Give me some names buddy, and then you can have your fix."

"Listen to me boss! Just look at me! I am half dead. Let me have it now – I will tell you everything you want to know after that! Please!"

In a minute, he was stuffing the gnaw into his mouth with shaking hands, washing it down with water.

And then, with an insolent smirk, he announced: "Fuck you now!"

Kolya served two years in a special narc prison camp – for possession only. If he gave any names, he could get from five to seven years for conspiracy and belonging to a criminal organization.

A narc prison camp was a rough place. The guards never interfered in inmates' skirmishes, no matter what they did to each other, the worthless junky scum.

Luckily, Kolya was able to use his charisma and fearlessness. He composed letters for a capo and inmates, and survived his detention with no major problems. I sent him warm underwear and a few rock'n'roll records, which in black market circles were called "disks".

When the capo saw what was in Kolya's parcel, he asked: "Are they disks or records?" After Kolya assured him that the parcel contained records only, Kolya played them on a funky record player he somehow managed to obtain, so everyone could enjoy Pink Floyd and Jimi Hendrix.

Two years passed and Kolya returned home. He had started all over again in a week. He made honest attempts to get off junk, but nothing worked. Kolya was desperate, but then a miracle happened.

He was able to break the addiction cycle by translating, from English, *Naked Lunch*, a book about the nature of addiction. Kolya believed that immersing himself into this delirious, funny, obnoxious and sometimes beautiful world of William Burroughs' imagination might help him to survive and get clean.

Somehow, it worked. Kolya kicked his drug habit, began drinking again, and translated into Russian a few of Jack Kerouac's books. He became a respected and popular translator.

He forgot the story of his arrest and his new friends didn't have a clue about many of his adventures.

But after all, were these stories really important?

The flux of living carried us further and further from these times and memories. So, what is next?

"Is that you again?"

"Yes, Kolya, it's me!"

SEARCHING FOR IRINA

A life merging
with a story,
a story morphing
into a life,
a dance and a dancer
unconcerned with gain
and loss slipping away
into the blurry beyond
leaving imprints
on dew drops only
hummingbirds can see.

Madeleine and Sausages

From the window of a reading room at the Lenin Library, I see the snowflakes swirling around yellow street lights. The lights are on for only a few minutes, but the soft, gray twilight already has sunk in the fresh, deep winter darkness. Cozy green lamps shine on every library table. A closed book is on my table. I strike the dark blue, old-fashioned, binding with my fingers. It feels soft and cool.

Golden letters on the front cover read: Marcel Proust, Remembrance of Things Past. I open the book. The print is beautiful and obsolete with some letters eliminated from the Russian alphabet after the Bolshevik revolution. Perhaps, it is the first Russian edition of the book.

At that time, I knew nothing about the value of first editions.

It is not an easy text to read, but I didn't stop until I read a passage my friend Shapovalov told me about this morning at school: "Just don't miss the madeleine (a shell-shaped cake) episode, then you will understand."

I put away the book and savor the passage. I never thought time had a taste that unlocked for Proust a rich layer of the past he pursued so relentlessly.

Vestiges of flavors not so subtle — of cheap port and a slice of sausage on coarse dark rye bread do the work for me. Images emerge in my mind and the past comes to live in me again. But is it a real breath of a rejuvenated life or just an obscene convulsion of a cadaver triggered by the galvanized power of a thought?

Starting over is a mystery and angst. The void of an unwritten story is mesmerizing. It can make one submissive, ready to be invaded.

But after you make the first decisive cut in the hardened skin of a memory, the fresh blood gushes out and new-born words burst into existence flooding a blank page.

Forty years later, and thousands of miles away I was am already sliding into the sweet morass of Morpheus when a thought in my fading daytime consciousness: tomorrow morning, after a hasty breakfast I will get back to my writing and talk to you again…

Can I Have a Beer?

That May morning in Moscow was glorious. The air was sweet and crisp. A few feathery clouds sailed lazily in the azure sky. Street-tough, ruffled sparrows jumped among fresh puddles and chirped vigorously. They were fat and happy.

Kolya, Soldier, and I sat on the stairs of an old bathhouse in downtown Moscow and peacefully enjoyed our beer. The entrance to the bathhouse was rather inconspicuous in the big, paved yard where a few strings with drying sheets stretched among dusty poplar trees.

However, the exact location of this entrance was well known not only to good citizens craving the rejuvenating power of steam. This bathhouse had a reputation for being the earliest morning beer dispenser in the city.

In that historical period, beer was officially not available in Moscow until 11 a.m. - the hour also known as Lenin Time. But there were some loopholes and exceptions.

Everyone in the country, including the omnipresent authorities, firmly believed that every decent human being older than 18 had a right to have a cold beer after taking a steam bath in a bathhouse. And they were opened before 11 AM.

A bathhouse has always been a formidable institution in Russia. For many Russians, it was the location of the weekly ritual they performed in the good company of friends.

For a newcomer, it might feel like heaven and hell at the same time. In the steam room, barely discerned in a cloud of hot steam, pink-skinned people lay on wooden benches or moved like ghosts, waving bath-brooms made of dried birch or oak branches. Every now and then, a respected specialist threw water from a bucket onto the burning-hot bricks in the big stove, and a fresh wave of hot steam filled the room. Bath-broom waving intensified, driving the heat closer to the skin. It was an amazing touchless massage accompanied by the refreshing aroma of dried leaves. Often, dried herbs such as chamomile and St. John's wort were added to the bucket, enhancing the healing power of the steam.

Every few minutes, steam-clad people emerged puffing from the steam room and jumped cussing, squealing, and laughing into a pool with ice-cold water. The skin was too hot for the cold to penetrate it. It was amazingly invigorating – I swear!

After the whole procedure was completed and all pores were open, one's body felt young and rejuvenated. And then, naturally, the thirst arrived to the relaxed practitioners.

The first bottle of cold beer acquired from a friendly steam-bath employee was a blessing. It was sucked down in one gulp.

Because of its irreplaceable role in the ritual, beer supplies in the best bath houses were substantial even in times of beer hardship. A bath house was a place where a knowledgeable thirsty citizen could find his early morning prize and remedy: a green half-liter bottle of cold beer.

The steps leading to the bath house entrance where I sat with my friends that morning was the place where I heard this ordinary phrase that changed my life: "Boys, can I have a beer?"

The one asking was an unfresh-looking woman of uncertain age with shoulder length thick, tousled black hair. She was medium height, slim, and had graceful hands with small, narrow palms and long fingers. Her fingernails were dirty and she smelled like sweat, yesterday's vodka, and cheap tobacco. Her swarthy face looked somewhat Egyptian with its classical proportioned nose, mouth, and a small chin. She wore oversized shabby blue jeans with a broken zipper, an old-style calico blouse missing a few buttons and beaten-up sandals. Her big, almond-shaped, dark eyes were foggy. She looked very vulnerable.

The beer we already had at this hour produced its pleasant and healing effect, and jokes we told in our small circle changed from dark to silly. Life felt sweet and easy, and comradery and love permeated the morning air.

Of course, she got her beer. I don't remember who bought it for her; most likely, it was always generous Kolya. It really didn't matter, because we were drinking together. We were not strangers anymore.

She introduced herself as Irina Nikolaevna, using the patronymic, which was usually used in Russia for a formal or official introduction. Kolya asked her permission to call her by her first name. She agreed with a chuckle.

Irina showed her quick wits and a keen eye for observation immediately after joining our circle. We had more beers, then switched to a cheap port we bought in an already-opened liquor store nearby.

The port tasted fine on that spring day. I can savor the vestige of that taste now as I touch my lips with the tip of my tongue.

Our eyes met for the first time when our gang crowded into an elevator, filling it with alcohol fumes and laughter. Freshly bought bottles tinkled in our bags. We were going to Kolya's apartment.

He was the ultimate host for all activities that evening because his lawyer mother, with whom he, strangely enough, coexisted peacefully, was out of town for the weekend. We had two comfortable rooms and the kitchen at our full disposal.

But the only thing I remember about that apparently successful party was the memory of Irina and me coming down in the elevator hand in hand.

We slept together that night at my place. We were very drunk. I held her slender body in my arms.

In the Beginning

There were many more nights we spent in my small room, which was jammed with an old German, upright piano, bookshelves and a desk – papers and books piled up on every flat surface.

We slept in the narrow bed I had since I was a teenager. There was enough room for us, and neither of us ever fell down. Like most of my friends at that time, I lived with my parents. Luckily, my room was right by the door.

We always arrived at my place after midnight and were as quiet as humanly possible. My parents slept in the bedroom right next to mine. We were separated by a thin wall and they somehow didn't hear any suspicious sounds coming from my room.

The gentle silence wrapping us was tantalizing. Every time our eyes or hands met, we felt deeply connected. Every subtle smile was a blessing, every touch was electric.

We sneaked out of my room usually before six in the morning when my parents were still asleep. We walked hand in hand to Kolomeskoe, the nearest subway station. We didn't talk much, just looked at each other, basking in the warmth of the past night. On the platform, I kissed Irina goodbye and caught the last glimpse of her smiling and waving to me from the departing train.

Then I took a bus home. I was back in time before my parents woke up. I was ready for one more morning performance. I didn't expect my parents to understand or to accept Irina becoming a major part of my world.

Disappointingly, most of my friends thought I had made a weird choice by getting involved with Irina, who was mercilessly battered by life and who was twelve years older than me.

Only Kolya and Dar accepted her right away.

"She's got a beautiful soul!" wise Kolya concluded when we spoke on the phone the day after our first meeting.

In the evening, I met Dar and we decided to have a few beers by the railroad tracks near his home. We settled on a small green hill near the tracks covered with blooming dandelions. The birds were singing, the passing trains were rumbling.

It was one of our favorite outdoor drinking places in the Sokol district where most of my friends lived. Thick bushes near the railroad shielded us from any prying eyes. Cops rarely showed up in that area.

We got two beer bottles out of my canvas bag, opened them with our keys and began the party. We spoke about Irina.

"She has got amazing eyes!" Dar shook his head emotionally.

"It was almost frightening! I felt I could drown in her eyes if I just looked at her long enough!"

The air of adventure was exhilarating around Irina – didn't matter where she was at the moment. And what an adventure she had!

Irina's turbulent life was abundant with trials and tribulations our motherland bestowed upon her so generously.

She was born in Istanbul to the family of a soviet diplomat. Her father was an ambassador in Turkey. Irina was two years old when World War II began. A few months after the beginning of the war, her father was summoned to Moscow with his family. He was arrested upon his arrival, proclaimed "an enemy of the people," and executed.

That was the fate shared by many soviet diplomats at that time. They were among the legions of people belonging to all strata of society ground to dust by Joseph Stalin's murderous machinery fulfilling his paranoid designs.

Stalin regularly purged his entire administration and power structures, so nobody could feel safe. Two of his supreme hangmen, chiefs of KGB, were executed by a shot in the head – just like their victims.

It was an approved method of execution in KGB cellars, thousands and thousands of people were murdered that way. The executioners had a plan they must fulfill; they received awards if they excelled. They had free vodka at work.

One day Irina introduced me to her friends, an angelic couple Nathan and Lisa. They were old artists and lived in a small apartment crammed with paintings, books and antique furniture, on the second floor of a sturdy, 12-story building built after the war, and located in Downtown Moscow. We visited them often after that.

I had noticed during one of our late visits that Nathan and Lisa shivered each time the elevator doors on the first floor slammed. They caught my puzzled look, and Nathan explained:

"The arresting agents usually came around this time. Many of our neighbors disappeared then. We always had a bag with soap, warm socks and a few other essentials by the door in case they would come for us."

They survived but never forgot the horrors of Stalin's time.

Nathan and Lisa were gentle, thoughtful people who didn't have children. They gave us plenty of love and wisdom. We cherished their company.

My own grandfather, Moses, told me a miraculous story of his survival at that time. He held a high position in the Ministry of Economics when the purges began. That made him vulnerable.

Amazingly, he built his career without joining the Party. He also was known for a short temper. The combination of both saved his life. One day, he slammed the door on his boss and was demoted. The person who replaced him was a party member. He was arrested a couple months later and perished in a Gulag. My grandfather was left alone because they were purging party members at that time.

Irina told me about another miraculous escape from the clutches of the KGB. This time it was a Jewish poet who survived The Night of the Murdered Poets when KGB agents rounded up Jewish poets and writers. None of them survived except for one who was drinking with a sculptor friend in his studio for a few days. Somehow, after not finding him that night, they didn't come for him later.

Perhaps even the Stalin killing machine was not perfect. Being drunk and unconscious was traditionally considered a virtue in Russia.

In the late 1990s, a film group had an experiment in Downtown Moscow. They filmed with a hidden camera as an actor pretended to be so drunk that he even couldn't open his car's door. Some charitable *babushka* helped him to unlock his car. Another passerby started the car for him. As the experiment proved, helping a drunk outweighed the damage he could cause by driving drunk.

I also had a friend whose father was an ambassador in Belgium at the same time Irina's father held his position. They were both summoned to Moscow at the same. Instead of returning to Moscow, however, my friend's father defected to France with his family. They returned to Russia later during *Khrushchev's* time in the early 1960s, so they all had a much better life than Irina and her mother.

Soon after Irina's father disappeared in the Gulag inferno, Irina and her mother were exiled to a remote village in Northern Siberia. They weathered the war living in an *Izba*, an old dilapidated log cabin half-sunk in the frozen ground. Irina's mother taught in the village school. Her students' parents brought her fish and frozen reindeer meat.

Irina picked cranberries at the edge of the marshes and mushrooms in the forest nearby during the ethereal, short northern summers. That was enough for the winter. Irina's mother also bought flour, salt and margarine in the village store.

They manage to endure six months of brutal winter and three months of darkness every year.

Irina told me about the Polar Lights the first morning we woke up together. I still remember her story:

"... A little girl in a calico dress, short of breath, frozen in wonder at the edge of the tundra carpeted with blue and yellow

flowers; her long, dark curly hair flying in the fresh wind blowing away a swarm of mosquitos. Her mouth is open, her big dark eyes gleam. In the sky above her, Aurora Borealis spread its iridescent morphing wings across the whole sky. Across the whole sky…"

Irina turned five years old in Siberia. That summer, Irina's mother met an Estonian man. He was just released from a Gulag camp nearby and was driving a truck for the camp's inmate logging gang.

He was arrested and sent to the Gulag in 1940 together with thousands of Estonians after Russians invaded and occupied their country. Latvia and Lithuania suffered the same fate.

It was the beginning of Stalin's ethnic cleansing campaign. At the same time when Baltic people were sent to Siberia, thousands of Russians were brought in to work in the newly built factories.

The occupation of Baltic States and Eastern Poland was codified in a secret pact between Stalin and Hitler. Soviet and Nazi troops paraded together in occupied Poland.

The Estonian Irina's mother had met was a good, reliable man, an architect in his former life. They got along well. He also was good with little Irina. They got married a year after they met and after Stalin's long-awaited death in 1953, moved to Estonia, that had been a part of the expanded Russian motherland for 13 years.

They settled in a small, old town by the sea, with narrow cobblestone streets and dark churches with long spires.

I was fascinated with Irina's stories. She was a consummate storyteller and had a deep, husky voice. Irina told her stories with a warm smile and cunning sparks in her gentle dark eyes. I could listen to her for hours, and hours we spent walking and talking during all four seasons through Moscow's winding streets and boulevards.

We stopped in cheap cafes and pubs for a beer, reinforcing it with port we poured into our glasses under the table. I perfected the under-table pouring skills necessary for any decent Russian wanderer during my college years, but Irina could do it much faster and more elegantly than I.

We usually carried a bottle of strong, cheap wine and a drinking glass in my denim shoulder bag. The bag was a reincarnation of my last worn-out blue jeans. The conversion was facilitated by my industrious cousin who made decent money tailoring fake blue jeans from the denim fabric and genuine looking buttons and labels he acquired in Lithuania. Sometimes the labels faded after the first wash but it didn't cause him much trouble.

We regularly resupplied our port, making our way through the city. We walked for miles, stopping in our secret spots in some back yards or secluded parks, partaking our wine on solitary park benches, or by railroad embankments when the weather was good. Old Moscow apartment stairways were our shelters in case of rain or cold.

After my graduation from college, I dreamed about going as far West as I possibly could. Considering my tainted reputation with the authority and my Jewish origin, Estonia was the furthest Western frontier available for me. It looked Scandinavian, people spoke a language similar to Finnish. They could even receive some Finnish TV programs!

I asked Irina during one of our first long walks:

"Why did you leave Estonia?"

"Because of Estonians."

"Don't tell me you hated them!"

"Of course, I didn't hate them, my sweetheart! I just couldn't live among them. They always spoke Estonian when Mother and I were around. It's an impossible language to learn, just like Finnish or Hungarian, it's not related to any other European language. I felt like an idiot sitting at the dining table and not understanding a single word they said. They never smiled at me, you know - Estonians really hate Russians after all that was done to them. I didn't have any friends there. My stepfather did his best. He was very nice with me. He was in love with mother for all these years and she loved him too. It was the best she could do – I was sent to Ukraine, to Odessa, to live with my grandmother."

Odessa is a beautiful city built in the late 18th Century. Many of its palaces and buildings have been influenced by the Mediterranean style, and look glorious under azure, southern skies.

Odessa always had been a multicultural, port city with a lot of character, a home for many famous Russian writers, musicians and artists, such as Bunin, Kuprin, Zoshchenko, Richter, Milstein, Oistrakh, and many others. People in Odessa speak a unique, instantly recognizable zesty dialect, a mix of Ukrainian, Russian and Yiddish. Odessa greeted sailors from all over the world with everything sailors could wish for – plenty of pubs and brawls, agreeable women, and contraband opportunities.

Odessa was the New Orleans of Russia. Every night, enthusiastic crowds packed numerous cafes and restaurants in the heart of the city where the bands cranked up spicy, jazz-like cabaret music.

George Gershwin's grandfather was born in Odessa. Odessa music possibly traveled across the ocean with numerous Jewish immigrants at the end of 19th century.

It was a great place to come of age.

Irina lived in Odessa happily with her grandmother. In the year she turned 16, she received a government letter from her stepfather informing her that her mother died from a stroke, and he was sending Irina some money.

It was 1956, the year when Khrushchev gave his secret speech denouncing Stalin and his cult of personality at the 20th congress of the Communist Party in Moscow.

It was the beginning of Khrushchev's Thaw. Soon after that, Irina received an official government letter exonerating her father posthumously. He was not "an enemy of the people" anymore.

Two years later, Irina finished school, received her passport and collected her money. She packed her belongings in one bag, and waved goodbye to Odessa and her tearful grandmother from a window of an Odessa-Moscow train.

Irina's bulky bag, a gift from her grandmother, probably was acquired before the Revolution. In the depth of this bag, squeezed between underwear and jars with grandmother's strawberry preserve, there was a bundle of school notebooks filled with quick but easy-to-read handwriting.

It was her poetry.

From the Life of Poets

We sit on a log by a red-brick wall behind a pile of lumber in the back yard of a ragged office building not too far from the Revolution Square in downtown Moscow. A half-empty bottle rests by our feet. Today we drink the amber muscatel from Crimea. It is as sweet as this quiet August afternoon.

It was raining in the morning, and a big puddle nearby reflects the gentle azure sky and a few stray clouds passing by.

A sudden gust ruffles a bundle of crumpled notebook pages. I nervously try to straighten them up. I am showing Irina my poems.

I pass her one page at a time and anxiously watch her reading it.

She reads it all in five minutes. She turns to me and smiles softly. I anticipate her verdict. I know my poems are naïve and wackily romantic.

She holds my hand and speaks to me with gently irony without being condescending:

"You've got some good lines here and there, but overall, it is too raw. I am sure, you can do better!"

She tussles my hair and kisses me on the lips.

"You are a poet alright, don't worry!"

Once again, she makes me happy. My very first critic happens to be a woman I love. I don't need to be defensive. Neither am I hurt.

Irina was the first natural-born poet I met. She and her poetry had very little in common with the writers belonging to the Writers Union and their work, the people who happened to be parents of a few of my high school mates.

The Union of Writers, as well as the Unions of Composers and Painters, was a pretty exclusive organization ingeniously founded by Joseph Stalin to keep tabs on creative people.

The members had to glorify our Socialist Society in styles approved by the authority. No denigrating Western influences were allowed. They were kept in line not only by fear of death, but also by generous perks: their work was broadly distributed all over the country. They were provided with special clubs with fine dining, special grocery outlets, luxurious housing and *dachas*. They enjoyed "for members only" fancy resorts that were called "Houses of Creativity" in the beautiful areas of our vast motherland.

Stalin handpicked loyal and zealous chairmen for each creative union with no regard of their professional capacities. He simply looked at their photographs spread on his desk and selected the most slavish and sleazy looking sons-of-bitches to lead their respective unions.

And what snake-tonged, heartless bastards they were! The chairmen ruled their unions with iron fists. They orchestrated condemnation of Shostakovich; the expulsion of Boris Pasternak. Many others suffered from their vicious oversight.

You could see them parading slowly in white pants and loose shirts along the magnificent Crimean embankments where the fresh sea breeze mixes with the fragrance of pines and cypresses. They walked slowly on the paths cleared from snow at the edge of dark woods blanketed with serene, winter silence. They looked like some human mushrooms in their wolf-fur hats.

Of course, there were some good writers, composers and painters belonging in these unions

But they were squeezed mercilessly by censorship, often inhabiting the children's section of the writer's union, which was less censored. Composers' escape was writing music for films. Painters stayed with portraiture.

Irina had nothing to do with poets belonging to the union who produced tons of patriotic, politically-correct garbage. The poets in her circle were perfectly antisocial and often very entertaining.

Once Irina and I decided to start our day at the huge, smelly pub near Belorusky train terminal. That's where I met Slate for the first time. The pub looked like a rundown warehouse and was built from corrugated aluminum.

The beer in the pub was dispersed from vending machines and was, like almost in any pub in Moscow, watered-down substantially.

We stood in a long line, winding among crowded "for standing only" tables jammed with beer mugs.

The majority of people in the pub were involved in under-the-table activities, passing to each other glasses and various bottles. Most people in the pub spoke loudly or screamed occasionally. It was as loud as an airport runway.

Suddenly I saw this tall, gaunt, unshaven man with long tousled hair approaching us quickly. He wore an elegant gray trench coat and slippers without socks. He carried a plastic bag with a large glass jar.

"Slate," he introduced himself to me shaking my hand and immediately addressed Irina in a conspiratorial fashion:

"Wait for me by this table. I know people here."

He headed right to the vending machines. After a short squabble with the thirty at the head of the line, he returned to us with three empty mugs and the jar filled with beer.

We poured the beer into our mugs, toasted each other with a clink. The party had begun.

"You look upset," Irina remarked smiling at Slate.

"Yes, I am!" he confirmed.

"I was peacefully masturbating in my study when my wife burst into the room screaming," confided Slate loudly.

"What a bitch!" he concluded sadly starting another beer.

"So, what's new?" Irina asked.

Slate put down his mug and straightened his back. He cleared his throat, clasped his hands. His gaze turned absent. He started to recite, rocking and popping his eyes:

Moi hui kak piyaniy stomatolg
V tvoe pluetsa gnilozubye…
My dick spits into your rotten teeth
Like a drunk dentist…

We ended this day passing out at Slate's apartment. His wife somehow was nowhere to be seen.

One day, Irina produced a yellowed, folded newspaper page out of her battered handbag. She carefully unfolded the page and handed it to me. It was a page from a five-year-old issue of "Lumberjack Daily."

"How delightful, "I uttered.

"Just read this," Irina pointed to a poem on the page.

Brodt, bruit po Frantzee
Obnishavshiy korol…
Wanders, wanders through France
One impoverished king…
The poem was signed; "Vadim K.

"What the hell!" I was amazed.

"That was exactly what a local reporter said after meeting Vadim in the lumberjack camp in Siberia."

I was puzzled. The newspaper looked like a typical provincial weekly full of pictures of lumberjacks posing with their chainsaws.

Irina enjoyed my confusion.

"That's what happened: someone saw this decadent poem published in this newspaper and contacted the editors. As a result, a reporter was sent to investigate this refined, poetic lumberjack. To his great disappointment, the reporter discovered that the new Siberian poetic wonder turned out to be a *tuneyadtetz (a parasite)* expelled from Moscow to Siberia. I know him. I used to belong to *SMOG*."

"You know Gubanov?"

"We can meet Lyenechka tomorrow if you want."

SMOG was something legendary for me. It was a notorious group of Moscow unofficial poets and artists. SMOG stands for The Youngest Organization of Geniuses.

SMOG's poets wrote dark, musical poems. They staged demonstrations by the Writers' Union club marching with funny satirical signs. They planted burnt-lime in the toilet bowls at the Writers' Union club, causing a huge scandal. And of course, many of them were arrested.

Lyenechka Gubanov was one of the founders of SMOG and universally recognized as the group's most infamous representative. He was a celebrated nomad of Moscow art studios and kitchens that were distinct salons of Russian intelligentsia. Soviet underground culture thrived in both venues.

I attended a concert of a popular singer-songwriter where almost 30 listeners were jammed into a very small kitchen. There were no complaints, and everyone was happy, including the songwriter, who got decent donations from the enthusiastic audience.

And it was a midnight kitchen gathering, lost somewhere in the undistinguishable geometry of Moscow's cloned apartment buildings, where I heard Gubanov reading for the first time.

We were sitting on the floor in a small kitchen together with a couple of dozen people, friends and strangers. A small table by the window was crowded with tea cups, glasses and various bottles encircling a loaf of bread and a plate with cut, smoked sausage. All eyes were on an attractive young man with short, dark hair and a dimple in his chin who had just swilled down a glass of cheap port.

Gubanov began reading, still holding the empty glass:

Zdravstvui osen – notniy grob,
Zheltiy dom moey pechali…
Hello autumn, a casket covered with notes,
An asylum of my sadness…

He was not published during his lifetime, except for a few poems published in Pinoerskya Pravda (the soviet boy and girl scouts' newspaper) when he was a teenager. Gubanov participated in the Glasnost meeting in Pushkin Square, was arrested, and soon after that, placed in a special psychiatric hospital.

He died in 1983 at 37 years old, the same age Alexander Pushkin was shot dead in a duel.

The Pit

Love of the Russian classical literature in Russia in my time was almost universal, bordering on religion. Sometimes it manifested quite unexpectedly: in some sleazy pub, you could see a half-conscious wino who suddenly sprang to life and grabbed one of his unsuspecting buddies by the lapels bellowing: "You, motherfucker! You just say one more nasty word about Sergei Esenin (a beloved Russian poet of the early 20th Century) and I will smash your pig face!"

But in the case of the infamous Karamazov brothers, I had some doubts that their distinct names Dmitri, Ivan and Alesha were inspired by the love for our great novelist.

Nobody even remembered the brothers' real surname, and it was not clear that their alcoholic parents, who worked at the knitting factory, "The Red Knitter," had ever read Dostoevsky.

The Karamazov brothers were cab drivers and lived in large, unkempt rooms in the communal apartment on the second floor of a shabby four-story apartment building on Pushkinskaya Street, not too far from Bolshoi Theater.

Irina and I spent many wild days and nights camping in the brothers' rooms and drinking with some of the weirdest people you could possibly meet in Moscow.

The cause of this insanity was the location of the Karamazov's dwelling: it was situated just a few hundred feet from The Pit.

The Pit was the nickname of the ancient pub located at the corner of Pushkinskaya Street and Stoleshnikov Lane, not too far from the fenced, ugly headquarters of the Attorney General of the U.S.S.R.

The official name of the pub was Ladya, an archaic word for a boat, but Muscovites called it by its true soul name: The Pit. The vaulted, smelly cellar was a popular drinking establishment in Moscow, probably since the time of Ivan the Terrible.

The Pit was also famous for its *zakuska* (hors d'oeuvres) plates. For a meager 50 kopecks you could select various Russian beer fare: a herring sandwich, boiled shrimp, cheese and sausage, etc. The pub was also the closest to the Red Square and the Kremlin beer dispenser.

The pub was frequented by all sorts of people, including provincial visitors and the notorious gang of regulars, many of whom happened to be Irina's friends.

I had never been to The Pit before I met Irina because of the long line of people waiting to get in at any time.

"I think you are ready to be introduced to The Pit," Irina said one day as we were walking down Gorky Street near the Red Square.

And of course, when we arrived at our destination, there was a long line by the pub's entrance.

"Don't worry about the line, just wait for me here," Irina whispered.

I stood quietly by the iron fence separating me from the anxious, thirsty crowd watching Irina passing swiftly along the line to the coveted pub's doors, accompanied only by a few muted complaints – one more manifestation of our national respect for drinking ladies.

Irina knocked vigorously at the heavy metal clad door. The door slightly opened and the gloomy bouncer's face loomed in the opening. Irina uttered a few words and the door opened wider. She squeezed in. The door slam shut again.

In a few minutes the door was ajar and I saw Irina's head.

"Come here quickly!" she commanded. I followed her path along the line and got inside.

We joined the motley crowd sitting at the long, wooden table by the arched, ancient window where you could see the passerby's feet.

People made room for us on a long, wooden bench, and we joined the festivities. The table was engulfed with a thick cloud of cigarette smoke that could serve as a cover for all sorts of drinking activities: opening various bottles under the table, filling up glasses, passing them around, swilling the drinks and chasing them with beer.

"So, this is Irina's new boy?" the fat, bold man sitting next to us smirked.

I stiffened up, feeling I was on display.

"Shut up, Frog!" Irina responded sharply.

"Just don't pay attention to this old fart." Irina uttered a short laugh and hugged me.

I didn't have a chance to finish my first beer when someone handed me a glass filled with vodka. Irina smiled at me warmly. I grabbed the glass, exhaled dramatically and swilled down the offering, trying not to smell it. Blood rushed to my face, my eyes bulged, my heart pounded. I grimaced, but I didn't throw up.

"That's a good boy," Frog went on again.

This time Irina ignored him. She hugged me and gave me a quick kiss on the cheek.

"Somebody give him a sandwich," commanded Alexandra, a beautiful brunette sitting across the table from us. In a minute I was chewing on a herring sandwich. I was hungry and completely drunk.

I had earned my right-of-passage in The Pit. Irina was happy.

The gang of regulars we joined comprised seemingly incompatible individuals who somehow coexisted peacefully most of the time. They were grocery store clerks, underground poets and painters, factory workers, engineers, actors, accountants and unemployed *tuneydtzi* (lazy parasites) on the lam.

All that was equalized by two powerful distinctly Russian factors: the desire to defy the absurdity of mundane living, and the love of alcohol that helped to break free from the chains – of course, temporarily – more or less on a regular basis.

There were only a few taboos at The Pit and you never knew what to expect anytime you were there.

One day, Ivan Karamazov showed up in The Pit with a plastic bag containing a few small frogs. The frogs were still alive, and desperately kicked their little feet.

"I will buy four beers for anybody who swallows a frog," Ivan proclaimed with a wry smile.

Burkov, a man of uncertain age and occupation, seized the bag without saying a word, pulled out a poor frog by its leg, and dropped it into his wide-opened mouth.

"Not a big deal!" he said, slapping his drooping stomach.

"It's still croaking," he added grinning.

But Ivan was not finished.

Ivan stared at Burkov's little eyes and uttered slowly and clearly:

"I will add a bottle of vodka if you chew one."

And then, after a few moments of silence, he added gravely:

"Without beer to wash it down."

Now all eyes were on Burkov. He thought for a minute, scratching his forehead and rubbing his hands. He sighed, then pulled another kicking little victim out of the bag, put it in his mouth and chewed it down slowly.

"It is so gross!" Irina exclaimed. Other people grimaced, but soon everything was back to the business-as-usual drinking and talking. Burkov enjoyed his well-deserved beer and vodka.

Irina's friend, Alexandra, a hospital nurse, demonstrated another case of The Pit's nihilism.

Alexandra had long, straight black hair flowing below her round shoulders. Her face radiated severe beauty and reminded me of a Native American. She was tall, very attractive and rough.

One afternoon, she showed up at The Pit with Ninka, a bleak, docile blonde resembling an oversized moth. Ninka worked in a laundry and made extra money by giving blow jobs to the needy.

We already had some beers and shared a few stories when I noticed two Georgian men wearing their customary huge *kepis* sitting at the next table. They were staring at Alexandra, intensely devouring her with their oily eyes.

Alexandra felt it. She raised her regal head and stared back at the Georgians.

"You, crocked asses! Do you want to fuck?" she addressed them calmly.

The pleasantly surprised Georgians nodded enthusiastically.

"Ninka, go ahead!" Alexandra commanded.

Obedient Ninka stood up and approached the disheartened Georgians. After short negotiations, they headed out.

Forty minutes later, Ninka came back alone and silently put a purple, 25-ruble bill on the table. She was a good friend.

The party went on.

Tell Me Who Your Friends Are

"I will waste my heart for Svyataya Bogoroditsa (Holy Mary)," Arbasov said passionately. He crossed himself gazing intensely at the small, darkened icon depicting the Virgin that hung in the corner of his living room.

Arbasov always spoke slowly and laconically, never groping for words, uttering them one by one with precision and confidence. He was a well-built, middle-aged man with cold, piercing eyes and a crew cut. His hair was gray and thick.

One day, when I saw Arbasov lifting weights in the living room, I noticed his distinct shoulder tattoo. It was the Thief-in-Law tattoo. Arbasov caught my gaze and grinned, silently continuing his exercise.

Arbasov was *Vor v Zakone* (A Thief-in-Law), the highest rank in the criminal underworld – just like a Godfather in New Jersey or Palermo.

People with such a tattoo were treated as kings in Russian prisons. They could grant life and death to any other inmate. Imposters were killed mercilessly.

Arbasov was always immaculately shaven and dressed casually. He had good taste. The first time I saw him, he wore gray slacks and a rustic, white sweater his daughter Marina had knit for him.

It was in winter when Irina took me to Arbasov's home for the first time. He greeted us, gave me a strong handshake and looked me coldly and directly in the eye. I felt uneasy and looked at Irina. She smiled at me reassuringly.

Arbasov's daughter, Marina, was a pleasant, quiet blonde. She was Irina's best friend for many years and worked as a librarian at the Nekrasov library near her home, not too far from Pushkin Square and Boulevard Circle. We liked to drop by the library during our long boulevard walks. Marina usually managed to get me some forbidden books from the special storage. That's how I got acquainted with Nietzsche's *Also Sprach Zarathustra* and Teilhard de

Chardin's *The Phenomenon of Man*, and a few other dangerous books.

Irina and I spent some time in Arbasov's home every week, and every time we stopped by, he gave us some money.

"Now go and get yourself some food and liquor," Arbasov usually said, laying a customary Chetvertak, a 25-ruble bill, on the table. It was more than enough for a few days' supply of food and drinks.

In that time, a loaf of good dark rye bread cost eighteen kopecks (five cents), one kilo of beef was two rubles (forty cents) and a pint of vodka or a bottle of excellent Crimean champagne was three rubles, twelve kopeks (sixty-two cents.)

So, after we finished our shopping with Arbasov's money – normally in an hour, if the lines were not too bad – we came back with bags full of groceries and cheerfully tinkling bottles. Upon our arrival, everyone had a good drink, and then, Irina and Marina, both great cooks, prepared the dinner and set the table while Arbasov and I had more drinks and conversation.

Arbasov never asked for the change after our grocery trips. His generosity helped us to get by. At that time. Irina didn't work, and my junior engineer's salary didn't last us more than a week. Most of it was spent on alcohol anyway.

One day instead of giving us grocery money, Arbasov handed me a big heavy duffle bag.

"I want you to deliver it. You have to memorize the address," he said probing me with the cold intense gaze.

It felt eerie watching him burn a piece of paper with the address in the ashtray. Irina and I took off with the bag at once.

After we came back, Irina reported to Arbasov, "Everything is fine."

Arbasov stared at us piercingly for a minute or so and didn't say anything.

The bill he put on the table this time read "100 rubles." I had never touched such a bill before.

We didn't know – and never asked – what was in Arbasov's bag.

One morning, Irina decided to introduce me to Vadim K. He was her old friend, a SMOG colleague and a former lumberjack in Siberia. Vadim lived in Matveevskoe, one of Moscow's working-class suburbs.

It is late January evening. We sit alone in a cold electricka (an electricity-powered commuter train). Pale fluorescent lights in our car buzz and flicker. The train rattles, its brakes squeal and hiss before every stop.

I stretch my legs along the soft, black seat. Its top is ripped, probably with a knife; the yellow stuffing sticks out in a few places.

My head rests in Irina's lap. She tousles my hair quietly. I look at the car's window. It is completely frosted, but I still can discern the bleak, washed out lights of the stations we pass.

We decide to have a drink. I am up now, rubbing my freezing hands before getting a cold bottle out of my shoulder bag.

We have one glass, so we take turns drinking to our journey. The strong wine warms our hearts and bodies. We embrace in silence.

After the long, hissing, electric cracks, an alien-sounding female voice, barely audible in the hum of the oscillating feedback, announces from the car's speakers, "Matveevskoe."

We hurry to exit and soon walk across a field, down a path trampled in the deep snow.

The untouched serene white around us sparkles under the full moon. We can see our breaths rise, coiling in the icy air. The crispy snow crunches under our feet.

The huge, round, apartment complex looms at the edge of the dark woods. A few windows in the building still pour a warm, golden light into the night.

Vadim is waiting for us. He has a long, dark beard, wears glasses and is already drunk.

Vadim lives in a small apartment with a kitchen and a living room (also serving as a bedroom) on the top floor, the sixteenth. His living room is cluttered with bookshelves and odd furniture: an antique cupboard with a couple of tea cups and heavy beer mugs (most likely borrowed from a pub), a rickety dining table, a few plastic chairs, a bulky armchair, and a huge, ragged couch along a wall displaying a few abstract oil paintings.

The view from his apartment windows is hypnotic and ghostly: a few pale solitary street lights, the snowy field and the distant village with dark, squatting houses. The blurry lights of the city gleam in the distance.

Five minutes after Irina introduced me to Vadim, he glares at me and says calmly: "If you hurt this woman, I will kill you."

"Vadim, stop it!" Irina interferes, "You know nothing about him!"

"That's exactly why I made it clear for him."

We drink in the living room. Glasses and a few bottles wait for us on the empty table. Irina or Vadim periodically pull a book from the bulky, dusty bookshelves and reads a passage or a poem.

We toast: "To Rilke! To Ahmatova! To Khlebnikov! To Chekhov! "

We travel through the languid time effortlessly, drunk on words and cheap port.

I feel encapsulated in the translucent bubble. I sense the outside, but I cannot communicate. I see Irina and Vadim suspended in their shimmering envelopes. They raise their glasses; their lips move, I cannot hear a word but I understand everything they say.

Irina looks at me, her bubble is drifting towards mine. Our trembling globules, collide and become one…

The next morning, I wake up in Irina's arms. The bright sunlight pours into the window. Vadim is still asleep in the arm chair near the coach where we lay. The table is crowded with empty bottles and open books. The window has no curtains, so I see the glaring white sun in the pale blue sky. I have a headache, and check the bottles on the table. They are all empty.

The radio in the kitchen plays Mozart.

Kratovo

April in Moscow is the month when spring at last gets back to the business of transformation seriously.

The large snow piles by the roadsides begin to turn gray, shrinking under the invigorated sun. Dark, spring rivulets run along the curbs. You can place a match in one of them and watch it sailing all the way to the nearest drain. The fresh buds on bare tree branches pop open, exposing fresh, sticky green leaves.

Fur coats and hats, woolen scarfs and winter boots are expelled to closets and chests generously scented with mothballs

Of course, we got our feet wet on the way from the commuter train to Regina's *dacha*. Regina was a socialite and a friend of many underground artists and poets. She was a daughter of one of the official Soviet writers, celebrated by the authorities, who had given his sizable and comfortable *dacha* to his beloved daughter after divorcing her mother. After that he bought a bigger *dacha* on the other side of the railroad, insulating himself from the ridiculous scum such as Irina and the like befriended by his overly-bohemian daughter.

We navigated our way from the station, moving cautiously among snow piles and large puddles for twenty minutes or so. Then, at last, Irina pointed at the cozy looking, two-story wooden house encircled with cute turrets and terraces – the true Chekhov-style *dacha* – and said: "This is the Ark!"

The gates in the tall wooden fence were not locked. We walked, passing through the large, still frozen garden, and knocked at the house door.

"Oh, whom do I see!" exclaimed Regina and embraced Irina enthusiastically. She shook my hand with a warm smile. I immediately felt at home at her place.

Regina was a sweetheart. She was one of these voluptuous writers' daughters who made men's hearts beat fast. Her smooth skin was snow-white, her long, dark curly hair fell on her round, plump shoulders. Regina had full, sensual lips and spoke in a low, husky voice. She also looked very natural in her elegant, imported attire.

Regina served us tea and biscuits on fine china. Our wet shoes and socks were drying by the fireplace.

I decided to take a closer look at the paintings hanging on the guestroom's walls. They all looked very modern, as if they came directly from the infamous "bulldozer exhibition." That's how we called the very first exhibit of the unofficial arts in Moscow that was held outdoors and which was swiftly bulldozed by the diligent Moscow authorities.

I stopped in front of one work depicting two very soviet-looking, plump women picnicking on the perfectly green meadow by a stream winding to the edge of the dark, low, fir forest. Everything looked pretty plain and sterile. Big, red letters printed along the painting's borders read: DANGER!

"Hey, Irina! Look at this one!"

"Oh yeah! Life is so sweet in the country!" It is Bulatov, he's always very efficient." she grinned.

A few minutes later, Irina went to another room to make a telephone call. Regina studied me silently for some time, looking at me above her designer eyeglasses. Then she put away her cigarette, blowing a perfect smoke-ring, and said: "My sweet boy! You have found yourself a great lover! Now you have to take care of this very rare bird; she is a prize!"

"I know you will," she softly cut me off when I was just opening my mouth to respond.

Most of the time when we came to see Regina in Kratovo we joined a motley crowd of her guests already fully immersed into drinking and reading activities.

One morning after a particularly intense previous-night's party, we awoke on the carpeted floor in Regina's living room among other wasted guests. It seemed that everyone suffered from a splitting headache and was ready for the usual treatment. Unfortunately, everyone was broke because we had already partied for a few days. A beer expedition was postponed. The best minds in the gang desperately tried to find the fastest way to acquire money for the cure. After some prolonged collective suffering, Irina came up with a bold proposal.

"We can paint a nice sign for the nearby trade union resort! I saw the sign on top of their main entrance on the way here. It was almost entirely faded. They must open in a few weeks and I am sure, they can use a new sign and pay us for it!"

"Sounds like a good idea," Slate said, moaning and stretching.

"Do we have any painters here?"

After a minute of silence, Regina concluded: "Nah, there's no painters here today; only alcoholics."

"So what!" Irina persisted, "How can they figure that out? Let's do it!"

Irina and I were dispatched to the resort to solicit the job and, hopefully, get an advance.

We went directly to the resort's office where Irina did all the talking and I tried to nod with confidence.

"We represent the group of teachers and graduates from Stroganov Institute (the Major Art College.) We came to Krartovo on a field trip, saw the sign above the entrance, and this is our proposal…"

Irina was eloquent and confident, so the resort's manager couldn't refuse her proposal.

We came back with a contract and a small advance, so the expedition to the local liquor shop was dispatched immediately.

In the meantime, Regina was able to furnish a few brushes, canvas, paints and other useful resources left by some oblivious painters who had camped at her place earlier.

We waited until the expedition returned with the remedy, opened the bottles, had our first afternoon drinks, and the creative process began.

We stretched canvas on the floor and placed heavy books along its borders to keep it from wiggling. Vadim, who had worked as a carpenter in Siberia, put the primer on. Irina grabbed a brush, squeezed some green on it, and boldly made the first stroke. The rest of us quickly joined them.

Amazingly, our employer was not shocked when Irian and I presented our masterpiece to him.

And what a piece of work we produced! Three crooked and very green palms occupied the left corner of our masterpiece, the blue, uneven lake took the area on the bottom, and the yellow sun with a few wry sunbeams shone in the upper, right corner. The large, and visibly uneven, red letters on top read: "The Krartovo Trade Union Resort."

Amazingly, the resort's manager didn't mind the palms, even though the nearest palms to Kratovo were thousands of miles away somewhere in Turkey or Greece.

Many years later I saw our sign still hanging above the entrance of the trade union resort in Kratovo. Tattered and faded, it had withstood the onslaught of elements and time, clinging to existence at the very edge of oblivion.

I still remember our springs.

In the Woods.

We stand on an empty platform holding hands. The commuter train doors hiss and shut behind us with a dull thump.

The train whistles and speeds up, leaving the station. It arches gently on the curve and disappears behind the woods. Now the only sounds we hear are bird voices and the distant hum of a jet plane drawing a white, fluffy line across the serene, morning azure.

We follow a path across the field into the forest. Everything around is full of life: ants busying around their hills, butterflies and bees descending onto bluebells, pinks and snapdragons scattered in the tall grass. Blue-eyed dragonflies zip by close to our faces.

We walk along a little stream at the forest's edge to a small lake. We undress quickly, throw our clothes on the grass and rush into the gleaming water.

We swim and splash, stirring reflections of trees and clouds.

We embrace standing shoulder deep in the cool, dark water. I kiss you. Your lips taste like a lake.

We get out of the water and you lay down on the delicate emerald moss under the old pines.

"Let's proceed with the copulation in the Kratovo woods," you say with a hoarse voice.

The dark whirlpools in your eyes expand, drawing me in. All things around us swirl, losing their shape. The hot wave swells and crashes inside me. The light darkens in my eyes…

On the way back to the station we scratch our bottoms.

"Apparently the ants enjoyed my butt and mosquitos had a ball with yours," you chuckle.

'God bless these animals!" I respond.

The Asylum

"What do you make of it?" Oleg handed me a batch of crumpled Solntzedar labels. The labels seemed to be detached from wine bottles by soaking them in hot water.

"I think it's the worst rotgut I ever tried!"

"I believe they planted it. They squeezed it into the crack under my door when I was in the bathroom," Oleg became agitated.

I looked at Irina. She just shook her head.

Oleg was Irina's half-brother, a tall, fragile, blond man with dark, brown eyes. He was a theoretical mathematician specializing in two-dimensional topography, unbeatable in tic-tac-toe.

Oleg worked for one of the major research establishments. He was an elite scientist who was allowed to work from home and required to submit his results once-a-month in-person. He spent 10-12 hours a day working at his desk by the window. The neat stack of papers covered with Oleg's handwritten hieroglyphs was on the desk to the left. An ashtray overflowing with cigarette butts was to the right. From the window you could see another identical, gray apartment building a hundred or so feet away. In the narrow yard between the buildings, there was a playground with swings and a slide, and a few poles with lines for drying clothes.

Oleg stayed inside his cluttered, smelly apartment as long as his supply of alcohol and cigarettes lasted. He was a functioning alcoholic and had frequent bouts of insanity.

Irina came to see him a few times a month, took the garbage out, cleaned the bathroom, bought groceries with his money and cooked enough food to last him until her next visit.

"He can survive on rotgut and cigarettes for quite a long time," Irina told me. Oleg grinned holding a cigarette with his yellowed fingers.

"They just don't leave me alone!" Oleg chewed his lower lip, "What should I do?"

"You just stay home, don't open your door to anybody and everything is going to be alright," Irina said calmly, in a motherly tone, and kissed him on the forehead.

"Don't forget, the soup is in the fridge!" she yelled when we were on our way out.

Soup had always had been a staple in Irina's diet. She cooked it in large quantities in all seasons.

Irina was the thriftiest home maker I ever encountered. One week we managed to survive on 10 rubles only, and it was her soup that fed us.

We started that week with going to a butcher in a local shop where Irina requested three kilos of bones.

"You've got a big dog!" the butcher smirked.

"Oh yeah, this son-of-a-bitch is enormous!" Irina laughed.

"There is always some meat left on the bones," she instructed me after we left.

"These suckers are just too lazy to scrape all the meat from the bones," she added.

In addition to the bones, we bought two round loaves of dark-rye bread, a big head of cabbage, a small sack of potatoes, a few carrots, and a small bunch of parsley. The rest of the money we spent on three packs of the cream cheese, *Druzhba* (friendship), a small pack of tea, and margarine.

At home Irina cooked the bones on low heat for half-a-day in a large pot, then added sliced potatoes, carrots, and chopped cabbage, salt and pepper, paprika and bay leaves.

She served the soup after garnishing it with fresh, chopped parsley. It was delicious! On top of that, the soup could last for a week in the fridge.

For other meals, we had tea and bread accompanied by fried cabbage rolls stuffed with cream cheese.

The soup Irina cooked for her brother had beef in it. Oleg supplied the money for groceries.

"Is it enough?" he always asked in an apologetic tone handling Irina the money. Oleg was paid well for his math work and didn't mind her keeping the change.

Oleg was the only family Irina had in Moscow. Her estranged husband had disappeared without a trace when their child was only one year old. Irina was 19 years old then.

Irina proudly showed me a photograph of her daughter, Masha, a beautiful 12-year-old girl with huge almond shaped brown eyes, just like her mother had. She always kept Masha's photo in her purse.

Irina had left her three-year-old daughter in Odessa when her grandmother was still alive. Alexandra Pavlovna did what she always did so well: she reared little girls sent to her by their loving, but desperate, mothers.

Different winds blew over Moscow in the mid-1960s. In 1965, dissident writers Sinyavsky and Daniel were arrested and convicted in a show trial. Sinyavsky was sentenced to seven, and Daniel to five, years of hard labor in Gulag camps. Their sentences signaled clearly: the times have changed.

Soon after those trials, SMOG was hit as well. Irina's friend Vadim had to return to Siberia again for his lumberjack duties. Another friend of Irina's, a poet named Nadezhda G., was committed to an insane asylum while she was pregnant.

And then there was the trial of the four writers: Galanskov, Ginsburg, Dobrovolsky and Lahkova were sent to the Gulag for their involvement in *samizdat* (self-published, underground journals and literature) publications in 1968.

Nadezhda was arrested and sent to an asylum the next week after the trial was over.

It was still three years before Nikita Khrushchev was deposed in 1971 in the palace coup in Politbureau, the highest ruling body in the country. Brezhnev became a new First Secretary of the Communist party. The period of relative liberalization and tolerance also known as "the Thaw" was over.

"Sure, that woman was unstable. It is insane to revolt against such a powerful political system like ours; people who do it must receive some medical help," a young, prominent psychiatrist had met at a party years later told me, answering my question about Nadezhda.

Once Irina read to me four lines from one of Nadezhda's poems:

> *Vi mnogikh ubili, proklyatie!*
> *Ya veru, nedes i zhdu.*
> *Kogda generali NATO*
> *Po ploshadi Krasnoi proidut!*
> You killed so many, damn you!
> I believe, hope and wait
> For NATO Generals
> To march in the Red Square.

Soon after Nadezhda's ordeal, Irina lost her job in Korolenko Hospital, an old and venerable institution specializing in treatment and research of venereal diseases.

On that gray and cold winter evening we were on one of our walkabouts. We were running out of wine, not too far from the Red Square. We were walking along the Moscow River. It was covered with thick ice. The stinging icy wind blew into our faces. Ghostly pale, fluorescent street lights rattled, casting dancing shadows onto the snowy street.

After taking the last swig from a bottle I looked at my watch: the time was half past eleven – all stores were closed. The cold began finding a way inside our coats.

"What are we going to do now?" I asked rubbing my palms.

"There is a possibility not too far from here," Irina answered. We crossed the Big Stone Bridge and turned into one of the half-lit, narrow streets of Zamskovrechye (a place beyond the Moscow River,) the 700-year-old district of Moscow originally populated by merchants and craftsmen.

We walked for a while along rows of dark, squatting two story houses with narrow windows. Irina knew her way.

Finally, we walked through a gateway into a small yard.

"Give me five rubles," Irina said quietly.

I handed her a bill.

We came close to a dark window on the first floor. Irina knocked on the glass five times. The curtains moved. Someone was watching us.

A minute later, a wicket in the upper corner of the window was ajar. Irina swiftly squeezed the bill into the opening. A minute later, a hand with a bottle and a glass on top of it emerged through the wicket.

Irina picked up the purchase.

"We have to return the empty bottle because we are using their glass," Irina told me after we settled comfortably on the stairs in a warm stairwell nearby.

The merchandise we acquired turned out to be a bottle of Solntzedar (A Gift of the Sun), the roughest of all domestic rotguts. But if you hold your breath for as long as possible after having a swig of this formidable potion, it was just fine.

The strong drink warmed us and lifted our spirits.

"So, what was the most useful thing you ever did at Korolenko Hospital?" I asked lighting my cigarette.

"I was an ordinary assistant in the laboratory of experimental syphilis," Irina smirked.

"I helped to set up some important and useful experiments. For example, once we tested the compatibility of leprosy and syphilis. "

"Any luck with that?"

"Two lab goats who were infected with leprosy were also given syphilis. Poor things still died from leprosy without developing any venereal disease."

"It's time for another drink," I proposed filling our glass.

Solntzedar did its job. We felt good enough to recite poetry. I came up with a Mandelstam poem. Irina read her poem dedicated to one of her friends who was diagnosed with full-blown syphilis:

> Vot tvoi krest, Marinochka -
> Vse nesut po odnomu –
> Tizh neseyesh chetire!"
> It's your cross, my sweet Maria,

Everyone carries just one,
But you have to carry four!
(Full-blown syphilis detected by the Wassermann test was marked by three crosses.)

Irina couldn't stop thinking and talking about her last day on the job.

"My boss asked me to see him in his office. He stared at me for a while, clearing his throat. Then he said that he never had any problems with me. He just got a certain telephone call – so he hoped I would understand his situation. I handed him my resignation letter in a few minutes.

Irina was blacklisted by the KGB Some of her SMOG friends were arrested, a few locked in psychiatric facilities.

It was an ugly situation. A severe depression hit Irina.

For days, she stayed in her bed or sat on a window sill staring blankly at the bleak landscape outside: the endless blocks of identical grayish five or nine story apartment buildings, laundry lines with frozen linen, hankerchiefed *babushkas* wrapped in their coats braving the cold and still sitting on their benches by the building entrances, eyeing anybody walking in and out.

Marina Arbasova and I came to see Irina almost every day. We brought some groceries, Marina cooked and forced her to have some food. She also was able to talk Irina into going to see a doctor.

In a few days, she checked into a hospital. In three weeks, she felt better and returned home. But now she was on a mental roster in a district clinic. Anybody who ended on the roster after being diagnosed with depression or any other mental disorder stayed on this roster for good.

Nixon Is Coming

Irina's voice on the phone was tense:

"Let's meet at the Kropotkinskyaya metro station in one hour. It's an emergency."

"What's happening?"

Irina laughed nervously:

"I will tell you when we meet. Wait for me by the first car coming from downtown."

I hung up the phone. It didn't sound good. Now it was my turn be restless.

In one hour, I was pacing the smooth marble floor of the Kropotkinskyaya station – the prettiest of all the famed Moscow subway stations. The slender, flower-like columns touched the high white ceiling with their petals. The lights concealed in the petals were soft. The walls and the columns were covered with beige, marble plates. The station hall felt like an open, breezy space, though like all old Moscow subway stations, it was 100 or so feet deep underground and designed as an ultimate bomb shelter. It was used as a bomb shelter during World War II.

It was rush hour. The trains spilled crowds of people hurrying to get back home.

I was already waiting for half an hour when somebody grabbed me by the shoulder. I turned around and came nose to nose with Irina's smiling face.

"Sorry for being late. I had to pack a few things."

She adjusted a big duffle bag she had on her shoulder.

"I will carry it for you."

"Let's go outside to the boulevard."

We settled on a bench not too far from the arched entrance to the station. It was already getting dark, but the street lights were not on yet. The crowed spilling out of the station became thin. Sounds of voices, steps, and passing cars blended into the undulating hum. The slow evening air was imbued with the fragrance of fresh linden leaves and gasoline fumes.

Irina lit a cigarette and said with a perturbed grin:

"I got a call from my psychiatrist this afternoon. He wants me to check into a hospital tomorrow."

"What happened?"

"Have you read the newspapers or listened to the radio lately? Nixon is coming!"

"Do they think you will be demonstrating by the Lenin Tomb with a black anarchist flag?"

"It's not funny," Irina said quietly. Her fingers holding the cigarette were trembling.

"I don't care what they are thinking. I just know that someone wants to put me away. Just in case. The doctor said: 'Don't worry, Irina Nikolaevna! You will stay there for two weeks only.' The son-of a-bitch sounded as if he was offering me a stay at a Black Sea resort for free."

Irina decided to go into hiding for a while. We walked down the boulevard discussing a possible place where she could weather the visit of our major adversary's president.

In forty minutes, we walked into the Nekrasov library by Pushkin Square where Marina Arbasova worked.

"I don't think my father would mind you staying with us for a while," Marina said hugging Irina.

Fifteen minutes later we stood in front of Arbasov.

"You can stay," he said calmly after listening to Irina's story.

"An American president in Moscow, that's what we really need now," Arbasov shook his head grinning.

Irina was safe for now, but many of our friends found themselves on the government mopping list.

Soldier lived on the second floor and luckily saw two cops heading to his doorway. He waited for them to get in, and then jumped from his bedroom window and ran.

Nervous Ghera surrendered to his demanding psychiatrists the same day after he received the dreaded call.

God got by using his usual tactic: he stayed in during the entire ordeal and didn't answer the phone or open his door to anybody.

Dar was, as usual, apprehended by the vigilant police patrol in downtown. Being true to his rebellious nature, he resisted arrest screaming, "Screw you and your American boss!"

He spent two months in the psych ward, longer than anybody else.

Wise Kolya urgently left for a prolonged Leningrad voyage. The authorities there had their hands full chasing and apprehending local deviants

Osheinikov was honored by a *psikhovozka* (psych mobile) parking by his doorway. He opened the door, greeting two stocky male nurses holding a straightjacket. Osheinikov was given a choice of a peaceful surrender, which he accepted. Local bench babushkas enjoyed the sight of him being helped into the van.

An agile American president upset our government by an unscheduled appearance at the Central Farmers Market where he attempted to interact with our decent collective farmers selling their meat, fruit and vegetables.

"Now he can tell everybody how lean our chickens are!" Irina commented with a chuckle.

But what really pissed us off was the treacherous destruction of our favorite Pokrovskoye pub, a very popular drinking establishment in the norther part of Moscow.

The Pokrovskoye pub occupied a small wooden building with two wings and a petit turret in the middle. It could easily pass for a peaceful *dacha* that by some evil design was overwhelmed by obnoxious drunken hordes. It also had a large grassy yard where the thirsty could peacefully settle and enjoy their drinking activities and a soulful conversation.

The vending machines in the left wing dispensed beer. In the right wing, the machines bestowed cheap rotgut.

The pub was just a few tram stops away from my alma mater, the Moscow University of Aviation, and was adored by its large student population.

Irina and I always enjoyed going there in the early afternoon. After some time spent in line with the cheerful college truants, we filled the glass jars we brought with us, alternating between beer and rotgut. The original pub beer mugs were probably stolen in the first week it was open, so pub customers had to be creative figuring out what they might be drinking from. I saw that some people used tops of the tubes for carrying technical drawings. Some sucked their beer from plastic bags outfitted with a tiny hole.

We were happy to join the crowd sitting and drinking on the green lawn near the pub, enjoying our drinks, conversations, and the loose work schedule tolerated by the socialist system.

But all these bucolic drinking pleasures came to an abrupt end that year. The peaceful pub fell victim to Nixon.

"All right, all right, just calm down, I believe you!" Irina blocked the telephone receiver with her palm for a few seconds and quickly informed me:

"This is Slate. He is calling from Pokrovskoye. He went berserk completely and swears that the Pokrovskoye pub has disappeared."

Irina returned to Slate on the phone:

"Do you remember? We were there yesterday together and everything was pretty much in order."

Irina turned to me again:

"Now he's cussing nonstop."

"Why don't we meet him there this afternoon? The weather is fine, so we can enjoy a few beers outdoors. I can still call my work colleague and he will cover for me."

"Hold on, Slate! Just listen to me, we're coming to Pokrovskoye right now. We will be there in 40 minutes."

Irina hung up the phone.

"I don't know what came over him this morning," she shrugged.

We took the subway and then a tram to Pokrovskoye. We got off the tram and followed the familiar path along the wooden fences of suburban *dachas*. We turned the last corner and stopped aghast: the familiar landscape – the same houses and fences, a small pine grove nearby – was strikingly missing one thing – the Pokrovskoye pub.

We saw the lanky, solitary figure of Slate sitting on the rim of the brand-new sandbox. The grass field was freshly paved with asphalt. A few other sandboxes and slides, feeble young poplars and a couple of flowerbeds with forget-me-knots were stuck in the middle of it. A few small groups of people stood around gesticulating. Apparently, they were cussing.

We approached Slate.

"Now you see! It's fucking amazing! I came here around eleven, just before opening, and couldn't believe my fucking eyes: the pub was gone! There were only these crappy boxes, the stupid trees and a guy sweeping the fresh asphalt. When I asked him, 'Where is the pub?' the bastard simply responded, 'What pub?'"

Soon the rumors circulating among the pub's former customers were confirmed: Nixon was the one to blame. The rampageous drinking institution was visible from Leningradsky Avenue, a major thoroughfare leading from the Moscow International Airport directly to the Kremlin. Our thoughtful authorities decided that Nixon could see the pub from his limo, an unpleasant sight that could defile the otherwise pristine image of our motherland. The pub's fate was sealed.

When the Nixon disturbances were over, my friends returned to their homes from hiding and psychiatric institutions, but memories of the American president's visit haunted us for a while.

A few weeks after the dust settled, I dropped by Kolya's place. We had a few drinks and then he unsealed a new single just recently smuggled into Moscow: it was the latest Crosby, Stills, Nash and Young. Kolya put it on the platter of his turntable …

"Tin soldiers and Nixon's coming…"
"How did they know? It's about us!" Kolya shouted.
"It's about us!"
I looked at the record cover. It said "Ohio."
"Let's drink to Ohio," I proposed.
"Why not!" Kolya laughed.

The Door with No Handle

It was my second October with Irina. The fall was rainy and warm. Mushrooms in the woods grew like crazy. Crowds of Muscovites with baskets filled the commuter trains every weekend to pick them.

We decided to join the hunt on Saturday morning. I was late and hurried down the stairs of Beloruskaya subway station to our regular meeting spot by the World War II Monument when I saw Irina leaning against the wall in her shabby jacket and oversized jeans. She gazed vacuously at the stream of people passing her while grasping an old-fashioned purse with both hands.

She looked so vulnerable and my heart shrank, but Irina gleamed after seeing me. We hugged and kissed silently, and headed out to the train station.

One hour later, we got out of the train with the small group of mushroom hunters that quickly dispersed in the nearby forest. Everybody was on the way to a cherished, secret, site where the precious fungi waited to be harvested.

We looked for porcini or Royal Boletus on the soft green moss under oaks crowned with golden leaves. Seeing the porcini's formidable smooth brown caps sitting on powerful white stems was a cause for joyous celebration. They were the most valuable and delicious mushrooms one could find in our area.

In the ethereal birch groves, we found yellow chanterelles hiding under astringent brown fallen leaves. Vigorous clusters of taupe, gregarious, straw mushrooms nested on mossy stumps and logs.

We had good luck combing through our secret plantation by a small, marshy pond overgrown with reeds and cattails. In a few hours, we filled our baskets with redolent, multicolored mushrooms and settled down for a snack at the edge of the woods under a regal oak tree.

It was unusually warm for mid-October. The tangy fragrant air wrapped gently around everything: the silent forest behind us, softly-rolling, empty fields and a ghostly, dark village in the distance.

We ate hard boiled eggs, bread and sausage. I poured hot tea with lemon into a thermos cup and passed it to Irina. She drank her tea slowly holding the cup with both hands. We spoke very little that day.

I knew about troubles she had with her new neighbor. Until this summer, Irina had shared a small two-room apartment with a neat, elderly woman. She had helped her with various chores and brought her groceries. The quiet babushka often treated Irina with homemade pastries and turnovers. They were good roommates for three years. But after Irina returned home from hiding last spring, she'd learned that her sweet neighbor had died.

The old lady's room didn't stay vacant for long. The week prior, Irina had met her new neighbor who was a warden in a women's prison.

At that time, people in Russian communal apartments didn't choose their roommates. The local district authorities maintained a long waiting list of those who needed a place to live in the area under their jurisdiction. Whoever was on top of this list, or had enough money for a hefty bribe, was the one to move into the first available room.

Considering all of the possible and often incongruous roommate situations in communal apartments,

Irina and her new neighbor were the most impossible combination.

Now after having some tea and food under the low gray October skies, Irina broke the silence:

"I can't stand seeing this ugly bitch! She treats me as if I am already an inmate in her prison. She barks orders to me: 'Take off your shoes by the door! Clean the stove after cooking! Turn down your radio!' She never tells me if someone has called me."

Irina's voice trembled. A tear dropped into her tea. She buried her face on my chest. I embraced her.

"We can go to my place tonight. My parents will be back home from the *dacha* tomorrow evening. We will figure out something. If you want – I can stay at your place for some time and deal with the monster. Then next week, Kolya's mother is leaving for a business trip for two weeks. I am sure he wouldn't mind us staying with him during that time."

Irina calmed down a little, raised her head and said sadly:

"Let's sort out our treasures."

We emptied our basket onto the grass. The fragrant pile of fine mushrooms cheered us up. We pulled out our pocket knives. We removed leaves and twigs from the mushrooms' caps and cleaned dirt from the stems. We put sturdy chanterelles on the bottom of the basket. The straw and butter mushrooms went into the basket next, and finally, we topped everything with magnificent, regal porcini. We used a couple of fallen fir branches for decoration.

"It looks beautiful!" Irina smiled at last.

Now we were ready for the proud display of our trophies in a commuter train or subway. It was common practice among mushroom hunters who were often hopelessly competitive.

We solicited a sufficient quantity of admiring and jealous looks on the way to my home.

At home we cooked an exquisite porcini soup with potatoes, onions, carrots and fresh parsley. Out of all mushrooms, only porcini broth is transparent and not dark – that's why they are called white mushrooms in Russian. We sautéed chanterelles and butter mushrooms with plenty of onions, and pickled straw mushrooms with plenty of garlic, pepper corns, bay and black current leaves, and dill.

I had a bottle of vodka in the freezer. Now everything was ready for a true mushroom feast. I poured ice cold vodka into shot glasses and put a Beatles record on my record player.

"… all my troubles seemed so far away…" Paul sang.

We stayed at my apartment until the next afternoon, Sunday, when we took the subway to Irina's home station. It was a twenty-minute bus ride from the station to Irina's place in Beskudnikovo – a distant working-class suburb. It was raining. The bus was packed, so we decided not to buy tickets – there's was no room for ticket inspectors on board. All buses in Moscow were self-served: passengers had to drop money into the cash box and tear a ticket from the roll hanging above the box; however, surprise raids by ticket inspectors were very common.

The bus passed bleak, red-brick apartment buildings, warehouses, and industrial facilities where cranes and other idle equipment in barbed-wired yards were soaked in the rain. We passed along a large power plant belching out black smoke into the gray sky from three huge smokestacks, and an abandoned, disintegrating village not too far from it, crossed a small bridge and entered Irina's neighborhood: a lattice of identical, white, nine- and twelve-story apartment buildings.

Now the bus stopped every two to three minutes, letting people with bags full of groceries and other merchandise get off and hurry to their homes. Our stop was the last.

We walked into Irina's apartment on the twelfth floor and I immediately came face-to-face with Irina's new neighbor. She wore a brown bath robe and had hair rollers on her head. She was carrying a bowl of a smelly fish soup. A stocky, middle-aged woman, she had thin, blondish hair, deep-seated, small, brown eyes, and fat lips. The warden passed us in a narrow corridor without turning her head or answering my greeting. She left behind an air of disdain and smelly fish.

We made our way into Irina's room and she shut the door.

"Now you see - that's what I told you!"

"Yes – having her around doesn't promise anything good."

I put the beer and groceries we bought into a small refrigerator by the door. It was empty, save for a jar of molded strawberry preserves and a few sprouted potatoes. Irina turned on a little black radio sitting on a chair near her mattress on the floor. It was tuned to the "Lighthouse," a round-the-clock radio station that played a variety of music and broadcasted news every 30 minutes.

"Oh, I haven't seen it before!" I pointed at a sketch lying on the table.

"You can a look at a few more," Irina handed me her sketch book.

I settled down on the mattress, leaned against the wall, and looked at the drawings. They were expressive and raw, minimal and dark.

Irina cleared the rickety table from piles of paper covered with her handwriting and pulled out glasses, plates and silverware from an old, faded antique cabinet standing in the corner by the window.

Irina's room was big enough not to be cluttered with her possessions. Books were piled up by the walls and on top of a small wardrobe. There were three unmatched chairs and a cozy reading lamp with a green shade on the table. The lamp usually travelled to the area of floor by the mattress at night.

There were blue calico curtains on a big window and a light-green wallpaper on the walls. Two abstract oil paintings hung on one wall. A photograph of Irina's daughter Masha was attached to another wall adjacent to the mattress, together with post cards with Modigliani's portrait of Anna Ahmatova and Peter Bruegel's *Winter* from *The Four Seasons*.

Irina made cheese and sausage sandwiches. We had our supper with beer and Prokofiev's violin concerto on the radio.

We sneaked in and out of the bathroom without encountering the dreadful neighbor. I set the alarm for six in the morning. I had to be at work at 8 a.m. – there were rumors that my boss might show up around this time to inspect my team.

The next morning, we had a hasty tea. I kissed Irina goodbye and hurried to join the gloomy Monday morning crowd waiting for a bus going to the subway station.

That was the last time I saw Irina that year.

The White Street, Yellow Lights.

He went out of the heavy, cast-iron gate - swung ajar - and slowly walked down an empty street along the tall concrete wall guarding the institution.

The snow intensified. The gusty wind blew big, wet snowflakes into his face. Some of them stayed on his eyebrows and mustache, slowly melting and forming tiny icicles. Soon his feet began to sink in the fresh snow quickly piling on the curb. The street lights suspended from the black wires in the middle of the street rattled and swung, causing his shadow to jerk on the snow.

He came to a bus stop on the corner and looked back on the snow-covered silent street: "The white street, yellow lights, the Cuckoo's Nest behind the snow…" he murmured.

He looked at his watch. It was almost 8 p.m. Probably the next bus would not come soon. He reached into his coat's pocket for a pack of cigarettes and unexpectedly grasped a small book.

"Shit, how could I forget?"

He pulled the book out of his pocket and stared at it irritably, wiping the snowflakes from the cover with his glove. The book was Nine Stories by J.D. Salinger.

"Idiot!" *he murmured slapping himself on the head and stuck the book back into his pocket. He pulled a pack of cigarettes and some matches out of the pocket, and after a few failed attempts, was able to light a cigarette, carefully shielding it from the wind with his palms.*

He took a few drags on his cigarette and suddenly saw a bus approaching quietly – all sounds were muted now by the blizzard.

The bus door opened with a clatter. The bus engine growled cozily. He threw the cigarette into the snow and quickly got in. The door closed behind him and the driver glanced at him listlessly.

He paid the fare and settled by a frozen window. He pulled out the book again, opened it at random and read: "For reasons I'm not at liberty to disclose, I've disguised myself so cunningly that even the cleverest reader will fail to recognize me."

"A good writer can sometimes afford to be a smart aleck," *he thought.*

"Take the titles for example – 'For Esme with Love and Squalor' or 'Pretty Mouth and Green My Eyes'," *he chuckled.*

"I don't want to hide because I want to move freely," he smiled faintly.

I don't have a place to hide anyway, not after so many years have passed. The story is growing inside of me and spreading through my veins.

Only now, when she's with me for good, I can write.

The Search

It was February already and I was running amok among my friends and acquaintances trying to find any clue to Irina's disappearance. I stopped at Arbasov's a few times a week, I went to see Vadim in Matveevskoe and Regina in Kratovo. I tried to talk to Irina's brother, but he didn't let me in and communicated with me through a crack in the door. He had a serious episode and was hiding from some alien KGB.

I even paid a visit to Irina's neighbor. The warden unexpectedly invited me into her room. After studying me in heavy silence for some time, she said that she had no clue where Irina might be.

On the way out, I noticed a big, new lock on Irina's door. After this dreadful visit I exhausted all imaginable opportunities to find out anything about Irina whereabouts.

Full of joyless determination, I fell off the wagon. The blurry world around me shrank and condensed into some timeless blob reeking of alcohol, extinguished cigarettes, and vomit.

The only thing connecting me with the outside was the cycle of hangover pains forcing me to leave my apartment in search of booze.

Then after one more blackout, I discovered that I'd been drinking with Slate for a few days.

We began to drink in the morning at the same pub where I first met him. We didn't speak much. We both felt Irina's presence near us.

Suddenly Slate put down his jar, spilling the beer all over the dirty table. He stared at me for some time until his, foggy eyes sparkled.

"You should check all the cuckoo facilities, starting with Kashenko Psychiatric Asylum in Moscow.

"Why didn't you tell me that earlier?"

"Don't be ridiculous. You should've figured that out yourself. It's obvious – that's where they put us in case of any excessive deviation. They locked me there last spring for a month without too much ado. "

Slate got back to his beer.

"You are a fucking genius. I am off to Kashenko!" I exclaimed.

"You are a stupid son-of-a-bitch! You can't show up there shitfaced! They will call the police and banish you for good," Slate squeezed out the last sentence with a considerable effort and produced a lion's belch

"Just fuck off!" Slate waved me bon voyage with his jar.

I finished my beer hastily and took off.

On the way out, I stopped in the toilet, stuck two fingers deep into my throat and vomited, clearing my stomach. I washed my face with cold water and combed my hair. I bought mint candies on the way to a subway station and ate a handful of them.

Inside

I was standing in front of an information desk trying to control my trembling voice and shaking hands.

"So, you are looking for Irina R.," a nurse at the desk said in a languid voice.

"Are you a relative?" she inquired without taking her eyes from a register's page full of names and numbers.

"Yes, I am her brother," I said without hesitation and uttered a resounding old aristocratic name: "Oleg Golitsin," that was also Irina's maiden name. I really hoped he was not on their list.

The nurse raised her eyes from the register and stared at me for a few moments. I thought I detected some irony in her look.

"Yes, she is our patient. You can visit her tomorrow from 3 to 5 p.m. in building #4, third floor."

The nurse shut the register and looked at me blankly, not responding to my hearty "Thank you so much!"

The next day I arrived twenty minutes before 3:00 p.m. at building #4, which turned out to be the special women's ward. I joined a small group of visitors waiting by the locked door on the third floor. At 3:05 the door opened and an athletic male nurse let us in into a small hall. I got in first and the nurse sneered at the three vermilion carnations I had in my hand. He locked the door behind us and opened another one leading to the meeting room. I had noticed that doors in the ward had no handles.

The large, sterile room with white-gray walls and two barred windows happened to be the place I had been searching for so desperately for three months. It was the only place we could meet now in our city this Saturday.

A stocky female nurse entered the room and asked whom I want to see.

"You came to see Irina?" she said, studying me for some time.

"You are the first visitor she has since the time we got her. Are you her husband?"

"I am her brother."

The nurse smiled slightly:

"O.K., brother, I will send her here."

I never imagined myself being a bloodhound, but the strongest memory of that day I kept for many years was the smell of the meeting room: the nauseating smell of trouble, stale air, disinfected floor, and mercilessly-rewashed, thick, brown cotton robes. A few women in such robes emerged from one more unlocked door and joined their visitors sitting at the tables. The visitors unloaded their plastic bags full of sandwiches, fruit, bottles with mineral water, and thermoses with hot tea and coffee onto the tables, and the visits began.

I noticed a poorly, but neatly, dressed old couple. They quietly smiled watching their middle-aged daughter with an apparent Down syndrome slowly drinking hot tea from a huge cup with bunnies painted on it.

Everybody spoke in a soft voice, but all sounds in the room merged into an indistinct hum in my ears. I was waiting at the empty table for some time. My heart pounded and I couldn't take my eyes off the door leading into the ward.

Then at last, the door opened and smiling Irina walked into the meeting room.

"Hello, brother!" she said softly and took my hand. The carnations fell on the floor. Irina picked up the flowers.

"Thank you, they are beautiful!"

She gave me a quick kiss on the lips.

"The nurse didn't buy your brother story," she said gazing into my eyes.

"I knew you were looking for me," she smiled and caressed my hair.

Irina looked fragile and hopeless like a caged bird. Her dreadful brown robe was oversized. She didn't have socks and wore large tattered salad-green hospital slippers.

Irina caught my look:

"Can you bring me normal slippers the next time?"

I touched a large dark crow's foot at the corner of her eye.

"Do they feed you a lot of crap?"

Irina looked around and whispered in my ear:

"I often manage to spit the pills into a toilet bowl. You know – they watch us after we take the meds. I pretend that I swallow my pills and then keep them under my tongue until I can get rid of them in a toilet. If they catch me, they will look in my mouth every time when I take the pills," Irina rubbed her eyes.

"Or worse – they will add some shit to my medications list."

"What injections do they give you?"

"They gave me Aminazine (an antipsychotic neuroleptic drug) – as usual during my first two weeks. I was unable to tell day from night, I was a total vegetable. Then I had a break for a week, but they started it again after I refused to take pills and resisted a nurse stuffing them into my mouth. Perhaps I scratched her a bit," Irina's voice trembled.

"After that two nurses held me pinned to the bed until the doctor came and said that if I don't like my medications, he will add another one. Then they injected me with Sulphosine (a suspension of sulfur in oil). I was in a pain and couldn't move for a while."

"The fucking Nazis!" I hissed.

"Be quiet!" Irina put her fingers on my lips.

We both stayed quiet for some time.

"All right, now tell me the story."

"This bitch, my neighbor, set me up. She wanted my room."

"This stinking freak caused your being here! She should suck Brezhnev's dick!"

"Calm down. They are already looking at us," Irina said quietly.

"It was worse. She had me arrested."

"What for?"

"Illegal treatment of syphilis."

"Holy Shit!" I looked at Irina with admiration.

"I never told you about it. I didn't want you to be involved. Actually, I didn't fucking tell anybody about it!" Now she was angry. Now it was my turn to calm her down.

"Since the time I worked in the Korolenko Institute, I had a practice on the side. I made some extra money by treating syphilis privately. I also had some good experimental drugs I borrowed from the lab I worked at. I did blood tests as well. You know – not everybody who was exposed would like to visit a district venereal disease facility. They treat all infected wretches there as if they are criminals. They put their patients on some black list. You stay on this list forever, so it can be used against you at any time," Irina sighed.

"I treated some people in my room. I told all my patients about my bitch neighbor. I told everybody to hold on for a little while until I could find another room. I begged them not to come!

And of course, one stupid drunk bastard showed at my apartment door when I was staying with the Arbasovs. He banged on the door and shouted that he must see me. The bitch sensed that something was cooking and let him in. That was it – he explained to her everything. She had me arrested the next afternoon, just a few days after we spent the last night at my place."

We absorbed each other words like someone who was offered cold water after almost dying from thirst in a desert. It was an amazing treat but we still craved more. Two hours of the intoxicating conversation flew by like a few minutes.

And then suddenly we heard a piercing shriek:

"The time is up! Everyone must leave in five minutes!" A thunderous voice of a nurse sounded almost happy.

The visitors hastily rustled their plastic bags with treats, passing them to their loved ones who were still chewing on something with absent faces. The last gentle words were uttered, the last hugs and kisses were given to women in brown robes. Irina bit her lips and didn't cry.

In five minutes, they all were back in the ward. The nurse locked the door with no handle behind the last of them.

Still Life

When life leaves us a few hard choices, perhaps not too many of us can accept one of these choices graciously and even find certain benefits in the freshly acquired misery. But one can at least attempt not to resist fate and unavoidable circumstances and simply move on with the flux we're still stuck in.

I came to see Irina at the psych ward four-to-five times a week. In spite of the cuckoo's nest environment, the new routine turned out to be not all depressing. I even thought that nothing could prevent us now from seeing each other during the designated visiting hours. I waited for these visits eagerly and my heart sang when I hurried with my plastic bags down the already familiar street leading to the asylums.

I got to know the nurses and brought some chocolate; I also met practically all of the ward's inhabitants.

One of them was nick-named Clinch. She was a middle-age gaunt woman with a long Roman nose, thick, tousled, dark hair, and green eyes.

Clinch didn't speak, but every few minutes she folded and twisted her lips into a seemingly impossibly shape and produced a loud sound: "Phoo-phoo!"

Clinch didn't cause much trouble to anybody. She just paced unceasingly everywhere she could, stopping from time to time in front of someone. She looked them in the eye, said "Phoo-Phoo," and continued on her path.

One day, a nurse allowed me to sneak inside and take a look at the room where Irina stayed with five more women.

The room perfectly represented the spirit of the institution: bare, gray walls, a barred window with no curtains, and six metal screen beds with shabby nightstands by each. Two long fluorescent lamps hung from the tall ceiling.

The room was empty except for two women. One of them everyone called "Professor." She looked cultured and refined even in her brown robe. Professor sat in her bed with her back against the pillow and read a thick ragged book. I looked at the book's title – it was *The Possessed* by Dostoevsky.

"Professor, meet my sweet heart!" Irina introduced us.

Professor glanced at me over her glasses and smiled. Later Irina told me that she didn't have any family and no one came to visit her.

Another woman in the room was "Screamer." She stayed erect like a statue in her bed most of the time.

Once, when we were in the meeting room, I heard a chilling howl through the ajar ward door. I almost fell of off my chair. Irina saw my reaction and grinned:

"That is Screamer. She does it once in a while, but it's hard to get used to it, especially at night."

I telephoned Marina after my first visit with Irina. We came to see her together the next time.

The two friends hugged and cried a little, and then Irina told us in detail about her journey from her home to the Kashenko hospital.

"I was drinking coffee in my room on Tuesday morning, the next day after I parted with my engineer."

Irina put her hand on my knee.

"I was in a pretty good mood, writing something, when I heard a loud knock at my door. I thought it was my neighbor and began feeling sour. I opened the door and almost went into a stupor after seeing two policemen staring at me gloomily. One of them asked: 'Are you Irina R.?' I was able to nod. They pushed me inside of my room and the same shithead announced with a smirk: 'You have five minutes to pack. You are under arrest.' They didn't' say anything else, just waved a paper that was supposed to be an arrest warrant in front of my face.

"The warden was out in the corridor and watched them escorting me. She didn't say a word, but I already knew – it was her; the fucking bitch had ratted me out!

Babushkas on the bench in front of the building had a ball watching the police getting me into their *Lunohod* in handcuffs."

Irina laughed hoarsely.

"And then I was camping at the special female ward without any idea when and how I can get out."

"So how did you pull it off?" I interrupted her, expecting to hear something entertaining and useful.

"You never could listen to anybody for too long," Irina rebuffed me and squeezed my hand gently.

"My arrest probably was in the making for weeks. In jail, an investigator announced the charges: 'illegal treatment of syphilis.' I didn't deny anything, but proceeded with my "cuckoo" routine.

"I was already on the roster in the district psych facility with manic depression and paranoia. All I had to do was just show some fresh symptoms. So, while in jail, I began talking to my shadow. Remember Li Po: 'I put a jug of wine among the flowers and drink alone on the quiet night…'

"He invited the moon and his shadow to join him and figured out that the moon didn't drink and the shadow didn't say a word. So, they all just danced together."

"It's a pretty graphic interpretation of the poem," Marina smiled approvingly.

"Yes, graphic is the key word. I made this poem my diagnosis. I persistently addressed the moon and had some heated discussions with my shadow. I also danced with my shadow on a regular basis and demanded vodka to toast them both. My cell mates loved my show! I assume that the jailers contacted my psychiatrist. Two week later I was sent to the Kashenko hospital for the psych evaluation.

"You are going to the loony resort, baby!" A cheerful sergeant declared, escorting me from the cell.

Irina smiled. Her cheeks reddened and her eyes shone. I was happy to see her feeling better and getting her sharp sense of humor back. It felt like we were sitting in one of the midnight Moscow kitchens, drinking tea and vodka, and talking to our friends. I almost forgot where we were.

We all stayed silent for a while.

I tried to lighten up the atmosphere: "Do you know which is the tallest building in Moscow? KGB headquarters (a seven-floor formidable building in Lubyanka Square.) You can see Siberia from its cellars."

The women laughed quietly.

"It was interesting," Irina sighed and continued her story.

"There's only one facility you can go to for the psych evaluation in Moscow: the special criminal ward at the Kashenko hospital. I spent more than a month there…"

"Phoo-phoo!" suddenly a boiling tea kettle sound and moisture blew into my ear.

"Get lost, Clinch!" Irina said firmly, but not harshly. Clinch stared at me for a few moments and then moved on to the other end of the meeting room.

I still remember what Irina told us about her evaluation.

She was sitting on a lone folding chair in a sterile room with bright, fluorescent lights hanging from the ceiling. Seven or so psychiatrists with gloomy faces sat at a long table a few feet away from her, all wearing white medical robes and caps. They had her file, notebooks and pencils in front of them. Irina perched on her chair like a ruffled, unhappy – but defiant – sparrow, wrapped in her gray hospital robe.

The psychiatrists shot their quick questions at Irina like bullets from an automatic weapon. She had to answer immediately without thinking, and then another question flew into her face.

"What is the difference between wood and glass?"

"You can lick a big piece of glass with no trouble, but if you lick wood, you'll get a splinter."

"What do you think about the proverb, 'Don't spit into the well?'"

"You can't catch the spit when it flies out of the well."

"And what about another proverb – 'Don't sit in the other person's sled?"

"I am not crazy about Merezhkovsky." (an obscure early 20th century Russian writer who hated the Bolsheviks and their revolution; the proverb was the title of one of his books.)

I always admired Irina's brilliance and ingenuity and now, years later, I hope that her answers could help someone in our time when the KGB tightens its grip on Russia.

I can also recommend two books dealing in depth with the phenomenon of psychiatric evaluation: *The Good Soldier Svejk* by Czech writer Yaroslavl Hasek, and *Confessions of Felix Krull* by Thomas Mann. These books helped some friends back then to secure urgently required diagnoses.

These books, besides being very funny, confirmed the major guiding principle useful in any successful psych evaluation: you have to answer each question in such a way that they won't expect you to answer it. In other words – you have to amuse your judges. Brilliance of your answers will clearly indicate that you are totally insane – and that will make your psychiatrists happy. Like many other medical professionals, they are smug when their diagnosis has been confirmed – doesn't matter if it is cancer, diabetes, or schizophrenia.

Svejk, for example, saluted a portrait of the Austrian emperor immediately after entering the evaluation room. That was enough for the doctors to consider him a complete idiot.

I brought Irina both books, but she told me that she couldn't concentrate enough to read them.

Some days I had to share Irina's company with Vadim, Slate, and a few other friends who'd learned what had happened to her. We sat in a small circle in the corner of the meeting room and shared our stories, teased each other with critical comments, and laughed. It felt almost normal, as if we were sitting at a beer-soaked table in The Pit.

I don't know about the other visitors, but every time I came to visit Irina, I imagined switching places with her. It sent chills down my spine. It made me think twice about my intention to get on the psych roster, like most of my friends, to avoid the draft.

We had some light moments during my visits, but any time I heard my own laughter in the meeting room I felt that I had done something obscene.

The institution stood guard against joy.

Cold Sticky Darkness

The cold sticky darkness creeps into my heart. Shit, can I just stop being poetic? Maybe it's the same as what my engineer once told me: 'It's impossible to stop being Jewish.'

You just find a silver pin shaped like a lyre in the park – just like Ahmatova did – and that's it. You must submit to your destiny.

I would never have imagined I would be reading my poetry to the enthusiastic audience of one hundred or so psychiatrists. I was exhibited at their monthly conference. I recited whatever I could remember for fifteen minutes and they gave me a standing ovation.

I wonder what kind of scientific revelations I reinforced for these shitheads.

At least they allowed me to have some paper and pencils, short and blunt ones – so I wouldn't be able to stab myself in the heart. It deprived me of an opportunity to die like a true poet. It would be a great obituary: 'A poet, Irina R., died at the age of 33 at the Kashenko hospital after stabbing herself seven times in the heart with a pencil.'

If I were a man, 33 would be a perfect age for crucifixion. Were there any women ever crucified, or perhaps those Roman bastards didn't find us worthy of such a glamour?

Just think of this primal man's urge to stick something between our legs, or any other orifice they can find… The thorns… They nailed people to crosses and then, after they suffered enough, killed them with spears – just more phallic symbols.

All these ecstatic crucified blondes depicted in our glorious century by Dali or bikers' paraphernalia.... The sadist's dream comes true.

My ass hurts; there is no more good place to stick a needle there. Someone crucified with syringes – a good image for our time. I don't remember when I had normal sex the last time... My situation is getting worse. They are talking about transferring me. It can be anything, it can be Stolbi, that fucking nightmare. This son-of-a bitch who calls himself a doctor told me he can't release me because I don't have any able relatives in Moscow.

Is it Wednesday or Thursday? He is coming on Saturday. They don't let me use the telephone. He will be searching for me again. Why doesn't he break up with me? I only cause him trouble. I am just a miserable, insane woman...

How insane should one be to fake insanity? I talk to myself too much, it's another symptom.

Oh no! It's Screamer again! I feel like I can smother her with a pillow. The poor wretch! She's hurting and no one bothers to help. Her family dumped her here. How much more shit can the world give us?"

They are taking me away. I know – it's not a routine examination. They gave me my clothes. I am being transferred!

Once again, I see the street through the bars in a van. We're driving away, we're turning... Where are you?"

Summer. No Joy

It's hot in the train. My shirt sticks to the back of the seat where I am squeezed between two country women and their plastic bags full of groceries.

The next station is Beliye Stolbi (the white pillars). I get off and make my way through the thick crowd of fellow passengers. Now I stand in a long line of people waiting for the bus.

Two stray dogs walk slowly across the dusty square. Their big pink tongues hang from their mouths. The sun is merciless. There's not a cloud in the pale blue sky.

At last, the bus arrives. People in line barely wait for the passengers to get off and rush into the bus doors pushing and shoving, then throwing their bags on seats to claim them. The bus is packed. I am lucky to have a good standing place. A couple of people are barely hanging by the bus doors.

The driver announces: "Please release the doors. We won't go anywhere unless the doors are closed."

In a couple of minutes, everybody manages to squeeze in except for one babushka with a big sack. She has to back off and wait for the next bus – probably for a long time. The old woman waves her fist and spits onto the departing bus.

During the previous two years, while visiting a few friends who had surrendered themselves to their stone-hearted psychiatrists, I became acquainted with a few asylums. Most of my friends successfully beat the system and were awarded the cuckoo certificates protecting them from the draft.

There were officially considered relatively harmless. The public tolerated their strangeness and perhaps even felt some sympathy for them. They were just poor, sick wretches who simply needed to be put away for a time for an appropriate treatment.

But playing games with dedicated psychiatrists was dangerous. Irina's attempt to escape the watchful eye of Big Brother caused a disaster. She got lost inside the incomprehensible psych machine and was tormented by its gears and cogs.

It didn't take long for me to find out that now no one could give me any hint of Irina's whereabouts. In the Kashenko hospital they simply told me that she was transferred.

I figured out she must've been transferred to the dreadful Stolbi, and that was where I found her.

I got off the bus forty minutes later, together with a small group of visitors, and walked down a winding pathway to the asylum. The dry grass along the path was turning yellow.

The set-up was not that different from other psych institutions: a bleak meeting room, disturbed, sad faces of the officially mad and their visitors, a nurse screaming: "Irina, you have a visitor!"

The only difference I can recall was the color of Irina's robe: this time it was worn-out green.

The only days I visited her were Saturdays. The trip to the asylum took almost two and half hours, so I rarely could make it during the week. The stream of friends visiting Irina soon dried up. Only Marina Arbasova came to see her from time-to-time. I didn't think it bothered Irina much.

She began to withdraw deeper and deeper into herself, and didn't ask too many questions about life in Moscow. I was the one who did most of the talking.

Irina listened to my stories with a faint smile. She nodded slightly and sometimes gave a short laugh when she liked what I told her. She was still holding my hand. Her gentle dark eyes were foggy. Probably it was a result of the injections and the pills they fed her, or perhaps she began to lose hope. Irina was inside psych institutions for almost two years. She told me one day she had to adapt to their dreadful routine to survive it.

During my visits we spent the most of time sitting on a bench, holding hands and looking at the tree tops and the sky behind the barred window.

On that Saturday Irina didn't eat or drink anything I brought her. She just held my hand, looked at me and cried a little from time-to-time.

I watched her going back into the ward after we kissed goodbye. She walked slowly with her head down, wrapped in her oversized robe and shuffling her feet. She didn't look back.

Leaving Irina behind locked in the ward was never easy, but my heart was heavier than usual when I went home that day.

The next Saturday I didn't find her at the ward. A stone-faced nurse at the reception desk simply cut me off:

"I don't know where she is. You are just wasting your time."

Through the Fields

I follow a narrow path through the field. The hot afternoon sun burns above my head, but suddenly a fresh breeze stirs the thick July air and sets in motion the mercurial waves of tall grass and flowers.

Now the path goes closer to the edge of the woods where the part of the field is mown. I walk to a haystack and settle comfortably with my back against it. A blue-eyed dragonfly hovers for a moment near my face and zips away into the trembling air.

A fluffy white cloud blocks the sun for a minute. Its shadow slides swiftly across the undulant grass. I listen to the even drone of an airplane – a silver needle moves unhurriedly high in the pristine blue sky.

In the distance, a toy train rolls along the darkening woods – I can hear its whistle blowing.

I am walking back from Troitskoye – one of the most secretive and feared mental institutions where people can disappear for years, or for good. It's the end of the line for the Russian psychiatric Gulag.

There are no visits allowed there, no information is given to anyone. The hideous gray building with barred windows is surrounded by tall walls. The gates are locked. I couldn't detect any sign of human activities.

I feel sure that Irina is there. That is the only place where they could transfer her from Stolbi: Troitskoye, The Special Psychiatric Asylum. It is a psychiatric prison for the insane and political prisoners who are considered dangerous for the socialist society.

I had circled a few times around the building, trying to look inside the windows. I saw nothing, but I hope Irina saw me. I cannot do anything else.

It is time to go home.

On the way to the train station, I sit on a haystack, and have some cognac from my flask. It warms my heart and soothes my mind.

I know I am totally lost, but at this moment, I feel I am inside the picture with everything around embracing me.

I feel you near me, I can almost touch you. I have fog in my eyes.

Oh, Irina....

EPILOGUE

A few summers later I was awakened by a telephone call. I looked at my clock and cursed – the time was 8:30 a.m. and it was a Saturday morning. I picked up the phone.

The voice on the other end of the line made me jump from my bed with a racing heart

"Do you still recognize me?" And then – a short coarse laugh.

"It's me. I am at Kolomenskoye subway station and I don't have money for the bus."

Blood rushed to my head. I tried to collect myself.

"Wait for me by the entrance. I will be there in fifteen minutes."

I dressed hastily, grabbed a half-empty port bottle from the liquor cabinet, a glass, and a couple of apples, and rushed out of the door.

I saw Irina from afar. She was leaning against the concrete wall of the subway entrance. She was dressed the way she had been when we first met: baggy jeans, a faded calico blouse and brown sandals. But something in her appearance was hard to comprehend – she was probably twice the size of the Irina I remembered.

We hugged and kissed for some time without saying a word.

Then Irina said: "They made me fat. It's what their drugs do to people."

She sounded embarrassed.

"You made it! The rest is crap."

A strange smile appeared on Irina's face. We decided to go to Kolomenskoye, a nearby monastery and park on the high bank of the Moscow River.

We settled down by an abandoned church and an acacia bush, had some port, and ate the apples.

There was a large vegetable field and a water treatment facility on the other side of the river bending softly in front of us. The rows of identical apartment buildings loomed farther away.

It was still early and there were only a few other visitors in the park.

We didn't speak much, only looked at each other for a while. Irina's eyes were warm and gentle, but she looked unsettled. I thought she might be trying to remember, or to relearn, something.

I felt uneasy. Our meeting seemed to be not entirely real: she was right there, near me. I had dreamed about this meeting for so long – and yet, I felt as if I was still dreaming and we were separated by some transparent, viscous membrane that didn't let our words and emotions get through.

My parents were out of town, so we spent the rest of the day and night at my place.

The next morning, after breakfast, Irina said she must leave. She was staying with some distant relatives I had never heard about.

"Can you give me twenty rubles?" Irina asked with a faint smile.

I gave her the money and we walked together to the subway station. On the platform, I kissed Irina goodbye and then saw her smiling and waving at me from the departing train.

It was the last time I saw her.

For years I heard vague rumors about Irina's whereabouts. Some people claimed she was dead, but I couldn't believe that.

POSTSCRIPT

He sits on the cracked stairs leading to the bathhouse, together with a few friends, smiling and squinting. The gentle morning sun shines in the cloudless sky.

He takes a sip of his beer and drags on his cigarette. A few green beer bottles huddle next to him. He lets out a perfect ring of smoke and watches it dissolve in the air among the floating poplar cotton-fuzz.

Suddenly a gang of sparrows descends on an acacia bush nearby, causing a chirping ruckus. They are gone in a minute.

He turns and says something to his long-haired friend with the formidable nose. They both laugh.

A slender dark-haired woman approaches them cautiously and stops a few feet away from the stairs. She looks fragile and humble. Her clothes are oversized and ragged, but she moves gracefully.

Now she speaks to them. They stop talking and look at her for a few moments.

One of them hands her a bottle. They make room for her on the stairs and she joins their fellowship…

"It was the merry month of May…"

Careless and stubborn –
merging gazes and heartbeats.
No need to make sense.

Once touched, they stay touched
turn after turn – the skin and
the heart remember.

Always in concert,
love and loss switching places
lured by the same light.

A page from Irina's prison notebook

It isn't lavender,
It isn't perfume,
I smell in the cell
The prison-soup fumes.
I smell in the cell
Dirty rags, cheap tobacco,
I reek of T.B.
Like the last jail-bed sucker.
There's soot in the cell,
There's grit in the cell,
And lesbian lust
Smells sickly as hell.
I stare at the sky
That's squared by the bars,
I cannot remember
The cherry-tree flowers.
The grass in the spring
I've already forgotten,
I smell in the cell
My head's turning rotten.

A page from Irina's prison notebook

Now, I am all alone
Like a fallen star
That fell down onto the road
And won't last too long,

Very quickly, I will burn and
Light the forest with my glow,
I'm not sorry that I fell -
A new star kindles in the night

There's a blue star in the sky,
Burning bright above your path,
Burning bright for you alone –
You just have to find it,

Let it sparkle in the sky
Let it shine for countless years
May Allah protect it!
May Allah protect it! *

    The last stanza is a modified quote from Misha Feigin's song, A Ballad about Smoleskiy Grocery

Misha Feigin was born and raised in Moscow. He won the Thomas Merton Prize for Poetry in 2000 and was awarded the Al Smith Fellowship for Creative Nonfiction in 2002. His books include a novel, *Searching for Irina*, a free style travelogue *Tribal Diaries*, a book of translations, *Anton Chekhov – the Ironist*, and five books of poetry: *The Last Word in Astronomy, Abraham's Bagel, Skippers in Training, Cloud Letters*, and *November Ending*. Misha currently lives in Louisville, Kentucky.

Misha Feigin is known as one of Russia's premier guitarists. He released two albums on the state label, Melodiya. He has toured throughout North America and Europe and has released 14 CDs in the US, Germany, and Holland. He has released two CDs in Great Britain on Leo Records. Misha shared a stage and recorded with Elliot Sharp, Steve Beresford, Dave Liebman, and Eugene Chadbourne.

Made in the USA
Columbia, SC
25 February 2023